The Outsiders: God's Called-Out Ones

The Outsiders:
God's Called-Out Ones

A Biblical Look at the Church —
God's Ecclesia

Clyde L. Pilkington, Jr.

BIBLE STUDENT'S PRESS™
Windber, Pennsylvania

The Outsiders: God's Called-Out Ones – *A Biblical Look at the Church* – *God's Ecclesia*
by Clyde L. Pilkington, Jr.
Copyright © 2010 by Clyde L. Pilkington, Jr.
All rights reserved.

Originally published in the *Bible Students Notebook* (ISSN: 1936-936) © 1999-2006

Executive Editor: André Sneidar
Layout and Design: Great Adventure in Faith

Cover design by Clyde L. Pilkington, III

    ISBN-10:   1-934251-61-5
    ISBN-13:   978-1-934251-61-4

Published by:
Bible Student's Press™
An imprint of *Pilkington & Sons*

  P.O. Box 265
  Windber, PA 15963
  1-800-784-6010

For information on *Bible Student's Press*™ releases, visit
    www.BibleStudentsPress.com

For information on other Bible study resources, visit
    www.StudyShelf.com

Printed in the United States of America.

CONTENTS

And the things that you have heard of me among many witnesses, the same commit to faithful men, who shall be able to teach others also.

~ II Timothy 2:2

INTRODUCTION

When people learn the truth about Paul's apostleship and message, they often ask questions like: "What happened to Christianity?" "When did the church abandon Paul's gospel?" "How did we get into such a mess?"

The real answer to these questions is not to be found in church history. The answer is found much earlier than that – in the writings of Paul, our Apostle.

Where does the believer who follows God fit in today's religions? To which denomination or church should we belong? In this book we will look at our Apostle's last words as found in the book of II Timothy. It is here that we will find the final marching orders for the church. Understanding this letter of Paul is essential to knowing how to walk as

> *A vessel unto honor, sanctified, and meet* [useful, profitable] *for the Master's use, and prepared unto every good work* (II Timothy 2:21).

Members of Christ's Body, "the Church" – the *ecclesia* – are God's called-out ones. II Timothy is their true story.

WHAT IS THE CHURCH?

The entrance of Your Words gives light; it gives understanding unto the simple (Psalm 119:130).

The word translated "church" in many English versions is not, at first, easily defined or identified today because of the influence of centuries of religious tradition. If we would clear our minds of these traditions we would find that this Greek word *ecclesia* conveys quite a very simple truth.

Consulting dictionaries does not always prove helpful. This is because we naturally approach the definition of any word with our traditions firmly settled in our minds, and the producers of the dictionaries have usually done the same as well. This is not intended to be critical of them. After all, words in dictionaries are being defined in ways that they are currently being used. That's just the intention of most dictionaries.

Words mean things, and since we are seeking the true meaning of God's *ecclesia*, we will of necessity be consulting with *His* Word to find *His* definition. This is all that really matters to us, who study the Scriptures. After all, God knows what His *ecclesia* is, and His Word is the source of *"light"* and *"understanding"* regarding it.

COMMON DEFINITIONS

Your Word is a lamp unto my feet, and a light unto my path (Psalms 119:105).

Among the common definitions of the word "church," we find the idea of:

- a physical building, as in, "It's our turn to clean the church."
- an organization, as in, "We are members of First Community Church."
- a meeting, as in, "Church starts in a half-hour."
- a doctrinal system, as in, "I've spent all my life in the Baptist church."

These are all *non-Bible* churches. Therefore, dictionaries and other man-made reference tools can be of only so much assistance as we study the Scriptures; we should always keep in mind that they are just that – man-made. Ultimately, the premiere reference tool for any Bible study is the Bible itself, because the Bible has a way of defining its own words.

In all languages, it is usage which determines the meaning of words; and since usage determines meaning, biblical usage, certainly, always should determine biblical meaning. Therefore, we must acquaint ourselves with the Scriptures. We need not stumble around in the dark, for His Word sheds great light on our pathway. The more we read, study and learn the Bible itself, the more we will be equipped to know the meaning of Bible words, and to live our lives according to their context.

Let's let God define His *ecclesia!*

THE CHURCH, WHICH IS HIS BODY

O send out Your light and Your truth: let them lead me ... (Psalm 43:3).

Now let's look at some *Scripture* definitions of "the church."

When writing to the Ephesians, Paul tells us precisely what *ecclesia* is:

... the church [ecclesia], which is His Body ... (Ephesians 1:22-23).

Isn't that clear? The church, *"which is ..."* – and here comes the divine definition – *"His Body."*

We can now say, with all authority and confidence, just what the *ecclesia is!* It is the Body of Christ!

Isn't that so very simple? Just taking God's definition; taking God at His Word!

Now, Paul shows us that the reverse of this is also true:

And He is the Head of the Body, the church [ecclesia] ... (Colossians 1:18).

... for His Body's sake, **which is** *the church [ecclesia]* (Colossians 1:24).

There is that *"which is"* again! We have here the Body of Christ defined. The Body, *"which is ..."* and here comes the definition: *"the church."* The *ecclesia* is the Body, and the Body is the *ecclesia.* That locks things up with clarity, doesn't it? God has provided a clear definition and then back-defined it, to make it an iron-clad truth.

This double-ended definition will lead us to even more truth concerning the *ecclesia.*

For instance, how many "Bodies" does God have in this dispensation? Paul clearly reveals that,

> *There is one body* … (Ephesians 4:4).

"*One*" means "ONE." God has *one* single Body in the dispensation of grace. This Body is *"the church [ecclesia], which is His Body."* Since God has clearly taught us that the Body is the definition of His *ecclesia,* and the *ecclesia* is the definition of the Body, then we can say with all divine confidence,

God has but one church in this dispensation – ONLY ONE – and His church is the Body of Christ!

The church *is* THE ONE BODY OF CHRIST. God has *no other* church or Body today!

Membership in the One Church

We have learned from God that the church, or *ecclesia, is* the Body of Christ. In this definition we were also able to learn that this church is, therefore, the one true church of our dispensation.

How can one become a member of this one true church? How do we become members of the Body of Christ? Let's again consult the only source of ultimate authority – God's Word!

> *For as the body is one, and has many members, and all the members of that one body being many, are one body:* **SO ALSO IS CHRIST.** *For by one Spirit are we all baptized into one Body* … (I Corinthians 12:12-13).

This passage tells us that the *one Body* has a membership. One does not "join" this church. One is "joined" to it by baptism – not water baptism, but *spiritual* baptism, where God's Spirit unites us into Christ's Body. Thus, the *one Spirit* through the *one baptism* joins us together into the *one Body.*

Look at the passage again, with emphasis upon these truths:

> *For as the **body is one,** and has many members, and all the members of that **one body** being many, are **one body:** so also is Christ. For by **one Spirit** are we all baptized into **one Body** …*

We also see these truths in Ephesians:

> *There is **one Body,** and **one Spirit,** even as you are called in one hope of your calling; one Lord, one faith, **one baptism,** one God and Father of all, Who is above all, and through all, and in you all* (Ephesians 4:4-6).

Here is the seven-fold oneness that we have in Christ:

One Body

One Spirit

One Hope

One Lord

One Faith

One Baptism

One God and Father

This unity we have is with Christ, and with every member of His Body. The one Spirit, by the one baptism, placed us into the one Body. There is no other Body of God today!

This one Body is at the heart of Paul's message about who we are in Christ:

... many members in one Body ... (Romans 12:4).

... members of Christ ... (I Corinthians 6:15).

... members of that one Body ... (I Corinthians 12:12).

... members of the Body ... (I Corinthians 12:22-23).

... members of His Body ... (Ephesians 5:30).

Notice that in each verse we are said to be members. One cannot "join" this church. One is joined to it by divine calling. This church is made up of all the saints of this dispensation. What a wonderful privilege to be already *"members one of another"* in Christ, His Body, which is the church!

*For as we have many members in one body ... So we, being many, are one Body in Christ, and every one **members one of another*** (Romans 12:4-5).

*... for we are **members one of another*** (Ephesians 4:25).

We are gloriously blessed with divine membership! God has made us *members* of His *ecclesia!* Membership in *any* other "church" stands in competition and contradiction to God's present purpose: His one church, His one Body!

THE ONE CHURCH AND ITS ONE HEAD

We have seen that membership in God's one true church for today is: by one Spirit, by one baptism, placing us into the one Body – and, that *one Body* has a name.

> *For as the body is one, and has many members, and all the members of that one body, being many, are one body: so also is Christ. For by one Spirit are we all baptized into one Body …* (I Corinthians 12:12-13).

Look at that little phrase in :12.

> *… so also is Christ …*

Any body is identified with its head. My physical body is "me" – identified by others with and by my "head." God's *ecclesia* is identified by our Head as well. The one Body is called *Christ*. He is the Head and we are His members. Thus, we are in living union with the wonderful Lord Jesus Christ. We are the many-membered *Christ*.

> *… the church, which is His Body …* (Ephesians 1:22-23).

Why is the *ecclesia* called "His Body?" Because the Lord Jesus Christ is our living Head!

> *… Christ is the Head of the church: and He is the Savior of the Body* (Ephesians 5:23).

> *And He is the Head of the Body, the church …* (Colossians 1:18).

This, then, brings us to another aspect of the definition of the church. The one true church has but ONE Head, and that is Christ. There is NO OTHER Head of God's church. This is how we can identify the true church – by its Headship.

Now the question is, who is the head of "your church?" Are you satisfied with the Headship of Christ over His church? Or, do you desire to *belong* to another "church" – different from His – that has another head?

GOD'S CHURCH

As we study through Paul's epistles, we are able to glean even further fullness of the definition of the church.

Paul identifies the church as **GOD'S** church:

> ... *the church of God* ... (I Corinthians 1:2).

> ... *the church of God* (I Corinthians 10:32).

> ... *the church of God* ... (I Corinthians 11:22).

> ... *the church of God* ... (II Corinthians 1:1).

> ... *the church of God* (I Timothy 3:5).

> ... *the church of the living God* ... (I Timothy 3:15).

We now see Who the church belongs to: the one true church of this dispensation is the sole possession of God Himself. It became His possession through legitimate means – He purchased it!

> ... *the church of God, which He has purchased through His Own blood* (Acts 20:28).

Who purchased "your church?" If it wasn't God, then it's *not* **GOD'S** church!

Over and over in the verses above, the one true church is clearly identified as *"the church of God."* Believers commonly join the world in using such phrases as:

"my church"

"our church"

"his church"

"her church"

"their church"

"Jim's church"

"Mary's church"

"Brother White's church"

"Reverend Smith's church"

Whose churches are these? They obviously are not God's. If they are not God's, then they must be in competition and contradiction with God's one true *ecclesia.* Does this not bother you? How long will we pursue such an contrary course?

THE HOUSE OF GOD

Another way that Paul refers to the one true church of this dispensation is:

> ... *the house of God, which is the church of the living God* ...
> (I Timothy 3:15).

The *ecclesia* is God's house. The living God lives in His living called-out-ones. Is this not a glorious truth?

Paul goes on to say that we are:

> *a habitation of God* (Ephesians 2:22).

> *God's building* (I Corinthians 3:9).

Paul was working on a divinely appointed project: *Habitat for Divinity!* What a thought.

"God's building" – just think of it! God has a *"church"* building in this dispensation, and it is NOT made up of brick and mortar. Rather it is made up of the members of His *ecclesia*. Praise the Lord for the one true *"church"* building of God!

Are you satisfied with this simple truth? Or do you embrace another "church building" instead? Are you *"the house of God"*? Or do you attend a man-made building that has been fraudulently pawned off as *"God's building"*?

THE TEMPLE OF GOD

Another way that Paul describes, or defines the one true church is that it is God's temple:

> ... *you are the temple of God* ... (I Corinthians 3:16).

> ... *your body is the temple of the Holy Spirit* ... (I Corinthians 6:19).

> ... *you are the temple of the living God* ... (II Corinthians 6:16).

> ... *a holy temple in the Lord* ... (Ephesians 2:22).

That the *ecclesia* is the temple of the living God is clearly borne out by Paul in these portions of Scripture.

We are the temple, we are God's sanctuary; not a *man-made* building, but a GOD-MADE building, made up of His called-out-ones!

Notice how clearly Paul contrasts the human and the divine in this regard:

> *God ... dwells not in temples made with hands* (Acts 17:24).

That's a simple truth, isn't it? God does not dwell in *man-made* places!

Now consider the common language of Christendom:

> "It is good to be in the Lord's House today."

> "Please do not bring food or drinks into the Sanctuary."

> "It is nice to have God's House full today."

Do you ever speak this sort of religious jargon? Such talk denies the truth of the Scriptures that we have just considered!

TEMPLE WORSHIP

Let's consider an important implication from our last definition – that we are God's temple. We have clearly seen that the *ecclesia*, the Body of Christ, is the temple of God today. One of the key features of a temple is **worship.**

> ... *the temple of God ... and them who worship therein.* (Revelation 11:1).

This identity of the temple with worship is why Paul says,

> God ... **dwells not in temples** *made with hands;* **neither is worshiped** *with men's hands, as though He needed anything* ... (Acts 17:24-25).

Now, a question comes to mind: Are you *time-* and *place*-oriented when it comes to worship? Do you need to go somewhere to worship God? Do you need to go somewhere, at a certain time?

Do you attend a Sunday morning **"Worship** Service?" If you do, does this mean that you stand upon the ground of *ecclesia* truth delivered to us by Paul? Or are you, by your actions, denying it?

Again, the question is a simple one: Are you *time-* and *place*-oriented in your worship? Listen to Paul's words:

> *For we ... worship God in the _____ ...* (Philippians 3:3).

In this verse Paul tells us **where** we worship! Do you know what goes in the blank?

> *For we ... worship God in the spirit ...* (Philippians 3:3).

Is this the truth that you live out in your life? WHERE do you worship? Do your actions deny the reality of who God has made you in Christ? Are you God's *ecclesia* – His *called-out-one?* Are you heeding His OUT-CALLING in your life to worship Him *"in the spirit"?* Or are you a *called-in-one* – heeding a man-made IN-CALL to worship in man-made institutions, organizations and buildings?

Do these truths really matter? Do they really matter to God? Do they really matter to you?

WORSHIP IN THE SPIRIT

The spirit is *where* God's *ecclesia* worships the Lord.

This means that *every day*, in *every place*, and in *every action* we have been called upon to enter into worship. After all, WE are the temple of God, God lives in us, and we therefore are to worship God with and in *every* detail of our lives.

No wonder Paul made statements like:

> *Whether therefore you eat, or drink, or whatsoever you do, do all to the glory of God* (I Corinthians 10:31).

> *What? Know you not that your body is the temple of the Holy Spirit which is in you, which you have of God, and you are not your own? For you are bought with a price: therefore glorify God in your body, and in your spirit, which are God's* (I Corinthians 6:19-20).

> *And whatsoever you do in word or deed, do all in the name of the Lord Jesus, giving thanks to God and the Father by Him* (Colossians 3:17).

Then when Paul wrote, *"For we ... worship God in the Spirit"* he quickly followed that truth with a negative:

> *For we ... worship God in the Spirit, and rejoice in Christ Jesus,* ***and have no confidence in the flesh*** (Philippians 3:3).

Did you notice that there were two realms in that verse – *"in the Spirit"* and *"in the flesh"*? Two different ways of worship! In the same verse, what stands between these two realms? – *"in Christ Jesus"*!

If you GO somewhere TO worship the Lord, are you not – in reality – denying the truth of who you are *in Christ Jesus*? Are you not worshiping the Lord *"in the flesh,"* rather than *"in the Spirit"*? Hasn't someone corrupted your mind *"from the simplicity that is in Christ"* (II Corinthians 11:3)?

Moreover, what stands between the two phrases *"in the Spirit"* and *"in the flesh"* is not just the phrase *"in Christ Jesus,"* but *"rejoice in Christ Jesus."* Is Christ Jesus your PLACE of rejoicing? Or are you placing your confidence in fleshly, earthly things?

Are you enjoying the true temple worship of this dispensation? Or, is your confidence in a man-made imitation?

GOD'S CALLED-OUT PEOPLE

Looking at the Greek word used to translate our English word "church," *Strong's Greek Lexicon* gives the etymology of *ecclesia* as "*a calling out.*" The *Concordant Keyword Concordance* defines it as "*a called-out company.*"

As we study Paul's writings, looking for the "church" of this dispensation, we have a key understanding of what we are really looking for – "a calling out." Can we locate this concept in Paul's epistles? Indeed we can.

Let's take a look at Paul's first letter to the Corinthian saints:

> *Unto the* **church of God** *which is at Corinth, to them who are* **sanctified** *in Christ Jesus, called to be* **saints** ... (I Corinthians 1:2).

Notice how Paul identifies "*the ecclesia of God*" as "*them who are sanctified in Christ Jesus.*" The word "*sanctified*" means "set apart." God's *ecclesia* is a called-out people, set apart unto God.

Paul goes on to say that God's *ecclesia* has been "*called to be saints.*" He is emphasizing that we are a *called* group of people! The word "*saint*" means "one who has been set apart unto God." So, once again, God's *ecclesia* is a called-out people, set apart as holy unto God. They are those who have been given the divine out-calling.

So, if we are God's *called-out* people, just what is it "out of" which we have been called?

Let's take a look at Paul's first letter to the saints at Thessalonica:

> *For they themselves show of us what manner of entering in we had among you, and how you turned to God from idols to serve the living and true God* (I Thessalonians 1:9).

Paul spoke these words to a people he had just identified, only a few verses earlier in the greeting, as *"the church"* (I Thessalonians 1:1). Now, these Thessalonian believers were *called out* of something. From what were they call out? *"From idols"*! They were Gentiles called out of their *social, heathen, religious system!* Yet that's not all: not only they *called out* of something, they were also *called unto* something – *"the living and true God."* That's why Paul called them *"… the church … which is in God the Father and in the Lord Jesus Christ …"*

The true *ecclesia* is God's called-out people. We have experienced the out-calling from *out of* the Gentile religious system, and into God Himself – alone. What a wonderful privilege to have such a calling, to be delivered from the bondage of such man-made religious tradition and oppression.

THE ONENESS OF THE ONE CHURCH

Paul defined the church for us in Ephesians 1:22-23:

... the church, which is His Body ...

This Body has *"many members"* (Romans 12:4), some of whom now *"sleep in Jesus"* (I Thessalonians 4:14), while others are living scattered throughout the earth.

All these *"members"* make up the *"one Body"* (Ephesians 4:4), the one true *ecclesia* of this dispensation. We are all ONE, geography not withstanding! This is why Paul carefully phrases I Corinthians 1:2 in the manner that he does:

Unto the church of God which is at Corinth ...

This *"church of God which is at Corinth"* is not another "church" – another "body," another *ecclesia* – than the one which was spoken of in Ephesians 1:22-23. This is the exact same church – *"the ecclesia of God."* When Paul speaks in this manner – *"which is at Corinth,"* he is talking about that portion of God's *ecclesia,* that part of Christ's Body that currently lived at Corinth.

This *"church of God which is at Corinth"* is not a separate *ecclesia,* not a separate "body" of Christ. He did not call them, as many often would, the "Corinthian church" – but instead, *"the church ... AT Corinth."* Do you understand the difference?

There is only ONE Body, one "church," one *ecclesia;* but some of its members were at Corinth, while others were at *"Cenchrea"* (Romans 16:1), and various other geographic places, and yet others *"sleep in Jesus."*

Now, that is not all that Paul said in his opening greeting to the *ecclesia* AT Corinth. Let's continue:

Unto the church of God which is at Corinth, to them who are sanctified in Christ Jesus, called to be saints ...

The *"church of God which was at Corinth"* was made up of those who were *"sanctified in Christ Jesus, called to be saints,"* but again, that's not all he says:

*Unto the church of God which is at Corinth, to them who are sanctified in Christ Jesus, called to be saints, **with all** who in every place call upon the name of Jesus Christ, our Lord ...*

Did you catch the significance of that? The saints who lived in Corinth did not solely make up a separate *"church of God."* The portion of the *"church of God"* which was *"AT Corinth"* was ONE and the SAME church *"with all who in every place call upon the name of Jesus Christ, our Lord ..."*

You and I – here in the future, scattered to the four corners of the earth – are members together with those who lived in Corinth in Paul's day who now *"sleep in Jesus."* We are all members together of the one Body, the church!

THE LOCAL CHURCH?

Yet someone protests, "What about 'the Local Church,' there's a basic Bible truth that you've forgotten!"

Is the so-called "local church" really a Bible truth? We definitely hear so much about it in Christendom. The phrase is a standard part of the "Christian" vocabulary; but is it actually a Bible phrase or concept? From where did the concept of "the local church" come?

Let's step back for a moment. We know that the Scriptures clearly teach that the Lord has only one Body today (Ephesians 4:4), and we also know that this one Body is the church (Ephesians 1:22-23). We know that Paul addressed the saints at Corinth as *"the church ... which is AT Corinth."* The Corinthian believers were not "the church" in and of themselves – they were but *a part* of the church, yet they were MEMBERS of *"the church"* nonetheless. They were *"the church of God"* – that was AT Corinth.

Now, Corinth was a *locality,* and there were members of God's *ecclesia* there. In other words, *"the church of God"* was **in** a *locality.* In fact, it was (and is today) in many localities. So the idea of *"the church"* in a locality is not foreign to the Scriptures; BUT there was not "a" church at Corinth – it was "the" church that was there: *the* ONE church, the *ecclesia,* the Body of Christ. Now *there's* a basic Bible truth – *"the church, the Body of Christ"*!

The church which was at Corinth was made up of *every* member of Christ's Body in that locality. No member was left out, nor was any non-member included. This church was NOT a building, a meeting, a doctrinal system or an organization – it was just a part of Christ's Body; members of His body that happened to be at Corinth at the time.

Before Paul came to Corinth, the church was not there. In fact, that's why he went there: he brought "the church" with him, so to speak. He *was* "the church" – at least a member of it. He preached His gospel (evangel, *i.e.,* good news), and those whom the Lord called were "joined" to the *one* true church by the *one* Spirit's *one* baptism (Ephesians 4:3-6). Then when Paul left Corinth, he took the church with him, *but* – he also left it there.

What was true of Corinth was and is true of any given locality. Let me use myself as an example. When I moved to Windber, Pennsylvania "the church" was already here. It was here long before I ever arrived. "The church" here in Windber is made up of *every* member of Christ's Body who lives here. Now, granted, not *every* member may walk in the truth of their calling, but we are *"members one of another"* nonetheless (Ephesians 4:25). There was nothing to "start," nothing to "found," nothing to "plant" – only something to "be" (as, we are *"called to **be** saints"* – Romans 1:7). We were called to Windber to live, to stand and to walk in the truth of the one Body, *"endeavoring to keep the unity of the Spirit in the bond of peace,"* and seeking to enjoy the fellowship and the mutual ministry of the *"joints and bands"* (Colossians 2:19) of God's called-out-ones.

THE CHURCH – IN A LOCALITY VS. THE LOCAL CHURCH

Now, there *is* something that greatly hinders and opposes the life of the Head living through His Body in a locality: it is the so-called "local church." That which is represented by this phrase, "the local church," has no biblical basis whatsoever. There is a vast difference between *the church in a locality* and the man-made system of "local churches."

A "local church" is a man-made, denominational, sectarian organization that has litmus[1] instead of life. These "local churches," with their human "heads," divide Christendom into manifold schisms.

Any given locality may have many such "local churches" in it. One's personal sectarian preference will usually determine which of them is viewed as THEIR "local church." If one is a Baptist, for instance, then when he speaks of "the local church" he means an organization which is in harmony with his denominational doctrine. Litmus, not life.

"Local church" is defined in light of one's flavor of denominationalism, making even the word "local" in "local church" a misnomer. It is usually the norm on Sunday mornings for Christians to pass MANY "local churches" to get to THEIR own so-called "LOCAL church." In fact, one may well travel by automobile for thirty or forty-five minutes, maybe even an hour or more to get to their own version of "local church."

Does that sound "local" to you? Even if, scripturally, there was such a thing as a "local church," wouldn't the closest "local church" be *the* "local church?"

---

1. An English colloquialism: Any kind of social indicator used to classify someone or something either favorably or unfavorably.

"LOCAL CHURCH" LANGUAGE

Does the so-called "local church" system make any sense to you? If it doesn't, it is because it is not scriptural – it's all man-made.

This humanly devised "local church" is the meaning of the word "church" in all the following statements:

"Attend the church of your choice."
"How many members do you have in your church?"
"What does your church believe?"
"Our church is at Main Street and Broadway."
"Where are you going to church now?"
"We joined their church yesterday."
"It seems that we are always late for church."

Now let's think about these statements:

"Attend the church of your choice."

This is a common statement that some groups often ridicule, but in reality it is exactly what they do! They choose which variety of "church" *they* want to attend. They choose one that suits their *own* fancy, and if there are two or more "local churches" that are of their same brand of doctrine, they'll pick the one *they* like best, or in which *they* are most *comfortable*. Then after a while, when things do not go to their liking, *they* choose another one. Or, if they are enterprising enough, they'll plant *their* very own "local church." This assures that it will be to *their own* liking! – and this is all done in the name of "serving the Lord!" Yet, in reality it is self-serving and creates further division in the one Body. We end up splintering the splinters!

When will we ever wake up and see ourselves as who and what God has made us? When will we ever stop "attending church," stop playing "church," and simply BE the church?

"How many members do you have in your church?"

The true church has members scattered to the four corners of the earth. We have no way of knowing for sure who they all are; but God does! After all, it is *His* church: *"… The Lord knows them who are His …"* (II Timothy 2:19).

"What does your church believe?"

Sadly there are many creeds, confessions, articles of faith and doctrinal statements in Christendom; but the Body of Christ should believe the revelation found for us in Paul's epistles (Romans 11:13)!

"Our church is at Main Street and Broadway."

If that's your "church," then it is *not* God's! His church is not brick and mortar (Acts 17:24), it is not stationary – it's mobile! It's everywhere! It's at the grocery store. It's at the gas station. It's at work, it's at the hospital. It's wherever you and I or any other saints happen to be!

"Where are you going to church now?"

Well, God's church is not some place to which you "go." WE are the church! It's who and what we are. It's our identity, and we shouldn't let anyone steal it away from us.

"We joined their church yesterday."

We have all the membership we need in Christ! Forget the other man-made numbers games. Be satisfied with who and what God has made us!

"It seems that we are always late for church."

We couldn't possibly be late for church! We *are* the church!

ALL the "churches" in the above statements are "local churches," and they are ALL the wrong churches! Not a one in the bunch is God's! Do these things trouble you? If they do, what are we going to do about it? Why not follow God's command through Paul to *"come out"* (II Corinthians 6:17). That's who we are – God's *ecclesia,* His *"called-OUT* people!" "Come out" and enjoy being all that God has made you in Christ!

Can you see how man-made and sectarian the so-called "local church" system is? *God's* church can be found in localities all across the globe – but there is no such thing as a "local church" anywhere in the Scriptures!

CHURCH-ES

Another issue that often seems confusing to many is the usage of the word "church-es" in Bibles. If there is only one church, which there clearly is, then why is the plural form of this word used?

As we have seen in the case of Corinth, the saints are addressed as *"THE church of God ... which is AT Corinth ..."* Therefore the believers at Corinth were "the" church at Corinth – God only had one church there! It was also just as true that "the church" was at Thessalonica, and many other places, each of these localities having "the" church, the Body of Christ.

Identifying particular members of the *ecclesia* in different localities is accomplished through the plural word "churches." In other words, the singular usage of the word "church" (or *ecclesia*) speaks of the Body of Christ as a whole, while the plural usage of the word "churches" (or *ecclesias*) is used to denote the Body of Christ in its various localities. However, this is a far cry from the man-made divisions and organizations that are being pawned off as "churches."

For instance, when Paul returned to the cities where he had preached the gospel, they ordained elders in *"every church,"* that is, *the church in every locality.* "Every church" is a reference to the Body of Christ's plurality of localities, rather than the plurality of man-made "churches" within a certain locality. This can be seen clearly in a parallel passage. When writing to Titus Paul told him to ordain elders in *"every city."* Do you see the connection? *"Every church"* – *"Every city"*? The issue is that the one true church – the Body of Christ – is manifested in various localities, but there is still only one church in each locality! Each city had only one church, and *that one church was the members of the Body of Christ in that locality!*

(Reflect upon these truths and ask yourself these questions: How many "churches" are in my locality? Which one is the *true* church? To how many churches do I belong?)

Paul, when writing of the various localities of the Body of Christ in the region of Galatia, referred to them as *"churches of Galatia."* There were many different localities (*i.e.,* cities, towns, etc.) in the region of Galatia, such as Colosse, Derbe, Lystra, Iconium. Therefore, knowing what we know about the church, we now understand that this phrase was not a reference to different churches! Instead, it was a reference to the church in different localities!

Therefore we have:

the churches of the Gentiles (Romans 16:4).

the churches of Christ (Romans 16:16).

the churches of God (I Corinthians 11:16).

the churches of the saints (I Corinthians 14:33).

the churches of Asia (I Corinthians 16:19).

the churches of Macedonia (II Corinthians 8:1).

None of these are a reference to man-made organizations. None of these are a reference to multiple "churches" in a single locality. These are all references to the one Body of Christ in its various localities. The Greek word used here for the plural "churches" is the exact Greek word used by Paul for the singular *"church"* (Strong's #G1577), *every time.* There is no difference – the only distinction is locality!

Concerning this plural and singular usage of a word, Tom West offers us an illustration, using the word "fleet" as applied to the United States Navy. In its broadest meaning, "fleet" describes all the operational forces of the Navy and is therefore not pluralized. The other usage of "fleet" relates to the numbered "fleets" which are associated with specific geographical areas such as the "Sixth Fleet" in the Mediterranean and the "Seventh Fleet" in the Western Pacific. Any two or more of the numbered "fleets" are referred to as plural "fleets." Yet they are all also the singular "fleet" of the United States

Navy. Each of the "fleets" represents the "fleet" in different specific geographical areas!

So it is with *"the church of God."* In light of all that Paul has taught us concerning the *ecclesia,* one could not attempt to use such "churches" passages to justify all the man-made divisions and organizations being pawned off as "churches."

THE CHURCH IN YOUR HOUSE

There are four *"church in your house"* type phrases found in Paul's epistles. These phrases are not insignificant. In fact, it is obvious that God determined to emphasize them in His Word.

> ... *the church that is in their house* (Romans 16:5).

> ... *the church that is in their house* (I Corinthians 16:19).

> ... *the church which is in his house* (Colossians 4:15).

> ... *the church in your house* (Philemon :2).

This basic Pauline truth should not be overlooked. It was quite simple: converted households were the natural expression of the Body of Christ.

The home has always been the center of all of God's earthly plans and purposes, whether God is ministering through Israel or the Body of Christ. In the dispensation of the grace of God, the home is the embodiment of God's church (the *ecclesia*). Thus Paul's expression was, even unto the end of his writings, *"the church in your house."* The *ecclesia* is clearly *domestic* in nature; it is not *institutional*.

EXAMPLES OF *"THE CHURCH IN YOUR HOUSE"* TRUTH

The truth of the domestic nature of God's *ecclesia* is not limited to Paul's use of *"the Church in your house"* phrase alone. There are many examples of this truth that should be apparent to the student of Scripture. Here is a list of some of the passages that show the central place of the home in the natural expression of God's *ecclesia*.

And a certain woman named Lydia ... and her household ... besought us, saying, "If you have judged me to be faithful to the Lord, come into my house, and abide there." And she constrained us ... And they ... entered into the house of Lydia: and when they had seen the brothers, they comforted them ... (Acts 16:14-15, 40).

But the Jews which believed not ... gathered a company ... and assaulted the house of Jason, and sought to bring them out to the people. And ... they drew Jason and certain brethren unto the rulers ... (Acts 17:5-6).

And he departed from there, and entered into a certain man's house, named Justus ... And he continued there a year and six months, teaching the Word of God among them (Acts 18:7, 11).

... house to house (Acts 20:20).

And Paul dwelled two whole years in his own hired house, and received all who came in unto him ... teaching ... (Acts 28:30-31).

... Salute them which are of Aristobulus' household (Romans 16:10).

... Greet them who are of the household of Narcissus, which are in the Lord (Romans 16:11).

Salute Asyncritus, Phlegon, Hermas, Patrobas, Hermes, and the brothers who are with them (Romans 16:14).

Salute Philologus, and Julia, Nereus, and his sister, and Olympas, and all the saints who are with them (Romans 16:15).

Gaius my host, and of the whole church, salute you … (Romans 16:23).

… them who are of the house of Chloe … (I Corinthians 1:11).

… they who creep into houses … (II Timothy 3:6).

… Salute … the household of Onesiphorus (II Timothy 4:19).

… who subvert whole houses … (Titus 1:11).

When these passages are given the attention that they deserve, one can hardly miss the true domestic[2] nature of the Body of Christ. If fact, what we will find missing from the teaching of Paul, and from the account of his life, are any inference of the association of God's *ecclesia* with institutionalism. This is purely a concept of man-made religious tradition.

Paul's domestic pattern of the *ecclesia* is not to be confused with His evangelistic efforts – the heralding (preaching) of the gospel that was primarily public in nature. In this phase of Paul's ministry he utilized many public places (note the word *"publicly"* in Acts 20:20) such as synagogues (Acts 13:5, 14-50; 14:1-7; etc.), open-air (Acts 14:8-21; 16:13; 19-22; 17:22-31, etc.), courtrooms (Acts 18:12-16, etc), and schools (Acts 19:9-10, where he *"disputed"*[3]); but, once again, these public activities directed toward the lost are not to be confused with God's *ecclesia*, and what Paul did when he *"gathered the church [ecclesia] together"* (Acts 14:27).

---

2. Domestic: "relating to or used in the home or everyday life within a household" (*Encarta Dictionary*); "belonging to the house, or home; pertaining to one's place of residence, and to the family; as domestic concerns; domestic life; domestic duties; domestic affairs; domestic contentions; domestic happiness; domestic worship" (Noah Webster, *American Dictionary of the English Language,* 1828).
3. *Strong's* G1223 and G3004; "to *say thoroughly,* that is, *discuss* (in argument or exhortation)." Note that the definition's main emphasis is on *civil* discourse, or discussion, *not* contentious debate that leads to strife.

WHY *"THE CHURCH IN THE HOUSE"*: RELIGION

Why is the home emphasized in connection with the *ecclesia* in Paul's epistles? We will consider a few reasons.

Some would suggest to us that this domestic nature of God's *ecclesia* was just because it was so "primitive." The idea being suggested is that Paul did not have the concept or means to institutionalize the church, conveying that somehow over the span of "church" history this problem has been corrected.

However, the domestic emphasis of the church is due to the very nature of the Body of Christ. Paul could have easily done otherwise; he could have employed an institutional pattern for us to follow. However, Paul went firmly against the grain of religious tradition – even of his own Jewish one.

The two firmly entrenched religions of Paul's day both met in special "sacred" buildings dedicated specifically for that purpose.

One of these was the only religion ever ordained by God; we speak of Israel. They had the temple (and the synagogues). Some of the Jews who believed and followed Paul undoubtedly truly "missed" this aspect of their past religious culture and lifestyle. How easy it would have been for Paul to have substituted a "church house" and a "worship service" for Israel's religious temple worship – it would have been such a "natural" transition – but he did not. He did not give his Jewish followers a substitute for their possible religious "withdrawals." He simply brought them home.

Then there were the various branches of the heathen Babylonian religious system which filled the Roman world. They all had "sacred sanctuaries" for the sole purpose of conducting their religious activities. Paul could have made his former idol worshiping followers feel somewhat "at home" by mimicking these meetings, but Paul disregarded these practices altogether. Neither did Paul give his Gentile followers a replacement for their potential religious "withdrawals" either. He simply brought them home, too.

Paul's very manner of life with the saints stood as a testimony that the Body of Christ was **not** a part of Judaism or the multifaceted Babylonian religious system. In fact, the Body of Christ was not religious *AT ALL!*

"The church in your house" supported this gloriously liberating truth.

WHY *"THE CHURCH IN THE HOUSE"*: IDENTITY

Paul's pattern and emphasis of *"the church in your house"* also stood in harmony with his teaching concerning our true identity.

Paul taught that we ARE the church (Ephesians 1:22-23). He taught that we ARE God's building (I Corinthians 3:9), we ARE His temple (I Corinthians 3:16), we ARE His house (I Timothy 3:15), we ARE His habitation (Ephesians 2:22) – that's who we ARE – *that is our **identity!***

God obviously knew full well that the religious system would attempt to steal away our true identity. Our true identity is confirmed and protected in the Pauline pattern of *"the church in your house."* All around us there are those who would, in practice and speech, deny these great truths! Even most of those among us who profess to know in truth that we are God's building, His temple, His house, and His habitation will nonetheless deny it in speech and practice. Just listen to these endless phrases of denial:

"Where do you go to church?"
"Our church is over on the corner of South and Main."
"He invited us to his church."
"I really love going to my church."
"I see your church is getting a face lift."
"Hurry, we don't want to be late for church!"
"Would you stop by the church and pick up our offering envelopes?"

ALL of these are the *wrong* church! Not a one in the bunch is God's! Do such phrases not trouble the heart and conscience of anyone?

Paul's *"manner of life"* (II Timothy 3:10) with the saints stood as a testimony that the Body of Christ *was* the "church building" of God. *"The church in your house"* was in clear support of this important truth. Religious talk, like that listed above, all vanishes away in simplicity of the true domestic nature of the church. Don't allow yourself to be beguiled!

*But I fear, lest by any means, as the serpent beguiled Eve through his subtlety, so your minds should be corrupted from the **simplicity** that is in Christ* (II Corinthians 11:3).

WHY *"THE CHURCH IN THE HOUSE"*: RELATIONSHIP

Paul's pattern and emphasis of *"the church in your house"* also stood in harmony with his teaching concerning our true relationship to each other.

Our relationship within the Body of Christ is likened unto that of a family. In the book of I Thessalonians Paul describes his relationship with the saints as that of a gentle mother (2:7-8), a concerned father (2:11), and a loving brother (2:1, 9, 14, 17).

To Paul, the saints were not "social acquaintances." They were not "parishioners." Paul did NOT view his relationship with them as a religious one. He had a special and tender relationship with them (*c.f.* Acts 20:36-38; Ephesians 4:32; Titus 3:2; II Corinthians 2:4; 10:1; Galatians 5:22). He regarded them as members of his family!

Paul calls us:

> ... the **house** of God (I Timothy 3:15).

> ... the **household** of faith (Galatians 6:10).

> ... the **household** of God (Ephesians 2:19).

Paul spoke of individual saints, at times as:

> ... his **mother,** and mine (Romans 16:13).

> My little **children** ... (Galatians 4:19).

> With Onesimus, a faithful and beloved **brother** ... (Colossians 4:9).

> ... Phoebe our **sister** ... (Romans 16:1).

> Unto Timothy, my own **son** in the faith ... (I Timothy 1:2).

These are all family terms. Indeed, family terms are Paul's *greatest* form of speaking of our relationship to one another. This subject does not get the attention that it should, probably because of its very familiarity (brother and brothers [or, *brethren*] are used over 130 times by Paul in his epistles).

To Paul, "brother" was not a formal description or title; it was an attitude of relationship, of personal commitment to genuine family ties (I Corinthians 8:11, 13).

Paul not only taught this, he lived it by example, and one of the ways in which he manifested this great truth was through *"the church in your house."* After all, where is the natural place for families to be and gather?

The Pauline pattern of *"the church in your house"* is at the root of the phrase, *"given to hospitality"* (Romans 12:13; I Timothy 3:2; *c.f.* Titus 1:8).

The expression of family life is centered in the home. It is the primary place where family life is conducted. Is it not, then, the natural place for the expression of the Body of Christ?

Now granted, on occasion there are family reunions where we get the extended family together at some rented location. These can be wonderful times of family fellowship, but this is the exception, *not* the rule of family life and activity!

So it is with the church, which is His Body. There were times when *"the whole church is come together into one place"* (I Corinthians 14:23). These were to be wonderful functions of family reunion (with special instructions from Paul on how to behave in an orderly fashion), but they were not to take precedence over the primary expression of *"the church in your house."*

Paul's manner of life with the saints stood as a testimony that the Body of Christ *as* a family – *"the church in your house"* – is in clear support of this truth.

Thank the Lord for *"the **simplicity** that is in Christ"* (II Corinthians 11:3).

FORSAKING THE PAULINE PATTERN

When Paul uses the repeated phrase *"the church in your house"* does it have **any** special significance or meaning? Or, is it just interesting historical "filler?"

Are we to suppose that building a special building just never occurred to Paul or any of his followers? Or, did he completely reject such a firmly established religious practice?

Was not Paul a tent maker by trade? Was not Israel's first building a tent? Could he not have made a tent in which to "have church" – a tent like Israel's tabernacle?

Yet this is *not* what Paul did! Paul was not founding a new religion, and neither was the Body of Christ to be a part of one of the two established religious systems. The church, which is His Body, was something new altogether, but it was *not* a religion!

Paul consistently lived so that his *"manner of life"* would reflect the truth of his doctrine, and he taught us to do so as well. Paul's doctrine is intended to have results.

> But you have fully known my doctrine, manner of life, purpose ... Yea, and all who will live godly in Christ Jesus shall suffer persecution (II Timothy 3:10, 12).

The tradition of the Babylonian religious system has, for the most part, replaced *"the church in your house."* In the process, the organic nature of God's *ecclesia* has been replaced by man-made institutions and organizations. This all comes from a failure to follow the simple Pauline pattern.

> Wherefore I beseech you, be followers of me (I Corinthians 4:16).

> Be followers of me, even as I also am of Christ (I Corinthians 11:1).

Brothers, be followers together of me … (Philippians 3:17).

The Pauline pattern has been forsaken! Now, what shall those of us who profess to follow Paul do about this? Shall we faithfully follow Paul as he followed Christ, or shall we continue to follow blindly the traditions of men?

Moreover it is required in stewards, that a man be found faithful (I Corinthians 4:2).

Will we follow Paul as he follows Christ, or will we follow some other man?

ᴸIGHT VIEW OF RELIGIOUS TRADITION

ion can be a very dangerous thing. It can nullify the ᴏrd of God. It blinds us from seeing the actual truth oᴛ His Word. Believers have too long taken a light view of religious tradition.

Noah Webster defines tradition as "that which is handed down from age to age; the act of delivering into the hands of another."[4] Likewise, James Strong defines it as "transmission."[5] Paul, the apostle of the Gentiles, warns the believer against these traditions of men.

> *And this I say, lest any man should beguile you with enticing words ... Beware lest any man spoil you through philosophy and vain deceit, after **the tradition of men,** after the rudiments of the world, and not after Christ (Colossians 2:4, 8).*

Man's religious traditions are dangerous opponents to the truth.

> *Making the Word of God of none effect **through your tradition,** which you have delivered: and many such like things you do (Mark 7:13).*

Paul, himself, had been caught up in tradition.

> *... being more exceedingly zealous of the traditions of my fathers (Galatians 1:14).*

Could not this statement made by Paul have been made by many of us? Have we not been exceedingly zealous of the traditions of "our fathers?"

Have you ever questioned the traditions that we so willingly have followed? Why do we do the religious things that we do? Have we

---

4. Noah Webster, *American Dictionary of the English Language*, 1828.
5. James Strong, *Strong's Exhaustive Concordance*.

ever traced their origins?[6] Should we not, then, follow our apostle, abandoning such man-made bondage?

Try this: the next time that you do something "spiritual," something "for the Lord," ask yourself why you do it. From where is its origin?

Now, be forewarned, this pathway will not be an easy one. The religious crowd will surely object to a lifestyle free from religious tradition. Most of the opposition will likely come from your closest friends and family members who are blinded by these very traditions of men, traditions from which you seek and have found freedom.

Be encouraged! Jesus Himself faced the same opposition and challenge from the traditionalists of His day.

> Then came to Jesus Scribes and Pharisees … saying, "Why do Your disciples transgress the tradition of the Elders?" … But He answered and said unto them, "Why do you also transgress the commandment of God by your tradition? … Thus have you made the commandment of God of none effect by your tradition … In vain they do worship Me, teaching for doctrines the commandments of men" (Matthew 15:1-3, 9).

Be careful about taking religion's traditions lightly.

If we choose to abandon our own religious traditions, I'd say we'd be in good company with Paul, and with our Lord and Savior Jesus Christ!

---

6. For assistance in tracing common "Christian" practices see *Pagan Christianity* by Frank Viola (available through www.StudyShelf.com – 1-800-784-6010).

A FORGOTTEN TRADITION

Often, when we speak of tradition, there is one that we have forgotten. It must be remembered that there is another tradition, a godly one that we *are* to follow: the Pauline tradition.

> *Therefore, brothers, stand fast, and hold the* **traditions** *which you have been taught, whether by word, or our epistle* (II Thessalonians 2:15).

> *Now we command you, brothers, in the name of our Lord Jesus Christ, that you withdraw yourselves from every brother who walks disorderly, and not after the* **tradition** *which he received of us* (II Thessalonians 3:6).

We are to receive the traditions of Paul because:

* He Is Our DIVINELY Appointed Pattern.

> *And these things, brothers, I have in a figure transferred to myself and to Apollos for your sakes; that you might learn in us ...* (I Corinthians 4:6).

> *Wherefore I beseech you, be followers of me. For this cause have I sent unto you Timotheus ... who shall bring you into remembrance of my ways which are in Christ ...* (I Corinthians 4:16, 17).

> *Be followers of me, even as I also am of Christ* (I Corinthians 11:1).

> *Those things, which you have both learned, and received, and heard, and seen in me, do ...* (Philippians 4:9).

> *Hold fast the form of sound words, which you have heard of me ...* (II Timothy 1:13).

But you have fully known my doctrine, manner of life … (II Timothy 3:10).

- He Is Our DIVINELY Appointed Apostle.

For I speak to you Gentiles, inasmuch as I am the apostle of the Gentiles, I magnify my office (Romans 11:13).

That I should be the minister of Jesus Christ to the Gentiles, ministering the gospel of God, that the offering up of the Gentiles might be acceptable, being sanctified by the Holy Spirit (Romans 15:16).

Unto me, who am less than the least of all saints, is this grace given, that I should preach among the Gentiles the unsearchable riches of Christ (Ephesians 3:8).

Whereunto I am ordained a preacher, and an apostle, (I speak the truth in Christ, and lie not;) a teacher of the Gentiles in faith and verity (I Timothy 2:7).

Whereunto I am appointed a preacher, and an apostle, and a teacher of the Gentiles … (II Timothy 1:11).

- To Him Has Been Committed this Current DISPENSATION.

For this cause I Paul, the prisoner of Jesus Christ for you Gentiles, if you have heard of the dispensation of the grace of God which is given me to you (Ephesians 3:1-2).

Whereof I am made a minister, according to the dispensation of God which is given to me for you, to fulfill the Word of God (Colossians 1:25).

… A dispensation of the gospel is committed unto me (I Corinthians 9:17).

According to the glorious gospel of the blessed God, which was committed to my trust (I Timothy 1:11).

... The gospel of the uncircumcision was committed unto me ... (Galatians 2:7).

But has in due times manifested His Word through preaching, which is committed unto me according to the commandment of God our Savior (Titus 1:3).

This current dispensation and its message were committed to Paul as a trust. The word "commit" means "to give in trust; to put into the hands or power of another; to entrust; to put into any place for preservation; to deposit;"[7] "to deposit (as a trust or for protection), to entrust."[8]

The word "trust" means a "charge received in confidence; that which is committed to one's care; something committed to a person's care for use or management, and for which an account must be rendered."[9]

As we receive the truth of this dispensation, we also receive the very dispensation itself and, like Paul, become dispensers of God's grace.

... Which is given me to you (Ephesians 3:2).

... Which is given to me for you (Colossians 1:25).

O Timothy, keep that which is committed to your trust ... And the things that you have heard of me among many witnesses, the same commit to faithful men, who shall be able to teach others also (I Timothy 6:20; II Timothy 2:2).

Why was Timothy to commit his trust to men who were *faithful*?

---

7. Noah Webster, *American Dictionary of the English Language,* 1828.
8. James Strong, *Strong's Exhaustive Concordance,* Greek Lexicon #3908, #4100.
9. Webster.

Because,

> ... *It is required in stewards, that a man be found faithful* (I Corinthians 4:2).

We now have a trusteeship that has been committed to our own trust. We need to be faithful to Paul's pattern – Paul's tradition – and be ever so careful of the religious traditions of men!

Are we following Paul's traditions, or man's?

A SNAPSHOT OF THE CHURCH

Think back for a minute, if you will. When Paul went to a new city – say, Corinth, for example – as a rule, prior to his arrival, there were no members of Christ's Body there. He would preach *"the gospel to that city"* (Acts 14:21). Upon trusting Christ his hearers were made members of *the church,* which is His Body. In other words, *all* of the saved in a geographic area made up *the church* of that area.

Let's say, for example, that after some time at Corinth there were 25 believers – *"the Lord knows them who are His"* (II Timothy 2:19). *All* of these believers were baptized by *"one Spirit"* into *"one Body"* (I Corinthians 12:13). They were *all* made members of *"the church of God"* (I Corinthians 1:2) when they were *"sanctified in Christ Jesus, called to be saints"* (I Corinthians 1:2).

No one needed to form, start or plant "a church." All that needed to be done was to preach *"the good news to that city."* God did the rest. He formed, started and planted the only divine church that was there – the only *ecclesia* that was *His* – *"the church of God."*

We hear a lot from the religious system about "starting" and "planting" churches. From where did such talk come? Does this sort of idea support, or contradict the truth of *the ecclesia,* the Body of Christ? If there is only one true church today, and God "started" this church with Paul, then what is it that *we* would be starting? It would be a man-made organization that would stand in contradiction and competition with God!

Paul preached the good news to the lost. Some of them – a few of them – believed and were saved. At the very moment they believed *Paul's gospel (evangel),* they were made members of *the church,* which is His Body. *No* man-made organizations were needed, *no* forms to fill out, *no* governmental recognition to seek and maintain, and *nothing* for anyone to join! Not a "church," not a "fellowship," not a "society," not a "club" – NOTHING! Every saved person in Corinth was already a member of the *only* church that God would *ever* have in Corinth!

There were no business meetings, board meetings or "church" property. There was only the *"church of God."* Is that not enough? Why do we find it so hard to be satisfied with who and what God has made us in Christ? Can we not see the hand of the Adversary here?

Peter Lord, in his great work *Turkeys & Eagles,*[10] reminds us of an important truth:

> We are all in danger of falling into the same trap into which Adam and Eve fell. They were tempted to become something they already were. The devil said, "If you eat … you will be like God." They were *already* like God. Made in His image and in His likeness …

> If the evil one can keep us from knowing who and what we are in Christ Jesus – new creations, saints, the people and children of God – then he can tempt us to act, by making us want what we think we do not have.

> The Christian does not do in order to become. He does because he is what God has made him in Christ Jesus.

Be the church!

---

10. Available through www.StudyShelf.com, PO Box 265, Windber, PA, 15963; 1-800-784-6010.

⊂ყ 59 ∾

DIVISION ENTERS

Let's continue our thoughts about Paul's church work, using the believers at Corinth as an example.

Paul preached the gospel to the lost; they trusted and were made members of *the church*, the Body of Christ. Every believer was a member of this church, no exceptions, for one Spirit had baptized them all into one Body. Now this is the ground of truth that Paul taught the believers to live and practice – their oneness.

Yet suppose for a moment that someone came up with the idea to start *another* church in Corinth – a church *other* than the one that God already had in place. Suppose he thought that it would be very beneficial to organize people for various reasons. So, he selected a nice name for *his* "church" (denominationalism). He devised certain "articles of faith" that he thought ought to be stressed and emphasized in *his* "church" (credalism). He developed a nifty governmental system from which *his* "church" could operate (clericalism). He laid out a program for *his* "church" meetings (formalism).

Also since all the other religions had one, he carefully made arrangements to secure a "sanctuary" for *his* "church" in which to meet (heathenism). He registered *his* "church" with the office of incorporation, and with the office of governmental recognition. He set up a bank account in the name of *his* "church." He printed stationery, business cards, offering envelopes, visitor's cards and, of course, a nice sign – all proudly bearing the wonderful name of *his* new "church" (and it all bore *his* own name as well – "Rev. Sam S. Smith," or maybe it was just "Pastor Sam S. Smith"). Then he purchased ads in the Corinthian Chronicle Daily inviting all to "attend" and join *his* "church," especially his "unchurched" brethren.

When one stops and considers all of this in the light of divine revelation, it seems really strange and odd, does it not? Yet it is much more than that. A *serious* problem has just been introduced onto the scene of the life of *"the church of God at Corinth"* – *division!*

Pastor Smith, wittingly or not, has just planted division in *the church* which is Christ's Body. Pastor Smith and *his* "church" now stand in contradiction and competition with God's church. Are *all* the members of God's church in Corinth members of *his*? Does he have members in *his* "church" that are not members of God's? Now, not only do we have the problem of division, we also have the same problem that Israel had in its past – the *"mixed multitude."*

One thing should be obvious, there are now two churches in Corinth. One is God's church – a divine, organic organism. The other is man's church – a human, fabricated organization. One is true, the other is false. The *root* of such a *divisive religious system* was already at work in Corinth when Paul wrote to them.

> *Now this I say, that every one of you says, "I am of Paul;" and "I of Apollos;" and "I of Cephas [Peter];" and "I of Christ." Is Christ divided? Was Paul crucified for you? ...* (I Corinthians 1:12-13).

Do a couple of names in that passage stand out to you?

How about the first name – Paul. Is he not our apostle – *"the apostle of the Gentiles"*? Yes, he is; but it is wrong to use his name as a rallying point to *create* another division within the body of Christ! Isn't Paul the apostle of *every* member of Christ's Body? Do you say "I am of Paul" with implication of separation and division from the rest of the members of Christ's Body?

Or, how about that last name – Christ. Is He not our Savior? Of course He is; but it also is wrong to use His name as a rallying point to *create* another division within the *His Own body!* Saying, "I am of Christ" sounds very noble, doesn't it? Yet isn't *every* member of God's *ecclesia* "of Christ" – aren't we *all* of Him? When we make this proclamation, we implicate a separation and false division from the rest of the members of His Body!

We must never forget that we are *"members one of another"*! Anything short of *"the church, which is His body"* is not God's church – regardless of how large, fancy, modern or decorated it is!

Why not simply be content with who and what God has made us in Christ?

> *And you are complete in Him* ... (Colossians 2:10).

What more could we want or need? Let us heed Paul's warning which he gave to us in light of this completeness in Christ. This serious plea can be found only two verses before:

> *Beware lest any man spoil you through philosophy and vain deceit, after the tradition of men, after the rudiments of the world, and not after Christ* (Colossians 2:8).

Why not stand on the ground of who God has made us? *Nothing* more, *nothing* less.

"CHURCH, INC." RELIGION

Now, let's get down to brass tacks. The Body of Christ, as a whole, is deeply submerged in the snare of the Babylonian religious system! Oh, that God would open our eyes to see such a sad state of affairs!

This is not a situation that has just developed. This spoilage of the church began in Paul's day.[11] He warned of it often. It was later brought to great and evil heights by Constantine. Sorrowfully, there was little or no real change produced as a result of the "Reformation." In fact, the Body of Christ may be more religious, more entangled in the Babylonian religious system now than at any point in its history. The worst part is that many members of Christ are, by and large, ignorant of this captive corruption.

501c3 Religion

The government and our precious misled brethren who have come before us have led us down the primrose path that has ended in this bondage. We have our own Americanized version of the Babylonian system. We have "Inc." religion, of the "501c3" variety.

501c3 is the federal bureaucratic code given to churches and other religious non-profit organizations that meet governmental approval. Many dear brothers who are held by the religious system would deny that they are a part of it; but here is an honest and objective test: Are you a part of a religious "Inc.?" Are you a part of a "501c3?" Are you using the exact same system that EVERY OTHER religious group in the United States uses? Are you actually a part of the SAME SYSTEM against which you profess to stand? Are you members WITH THEM in this Gentile religious system?

Listen to our apostle, Paul:

---

11. For a detailed study of this early departure from the truth and pattern of Paul, read the author's book – *The Church in Ruins: Brief Thoughts on II Timothy*; available from www.ClydePilkington.com, PO Box 265 Windber, PA 15963, 1-800-784-6010.

*Be not unequally yoked together with unbelievers: for what fellowship has righteousness with unrighteousness? And what communion has light with darkness? And what concord has Christ with Belial? Or what part has he who believes with an infidel? And what agreement has the temple of God with idols? For you are the temple of the living God; as God has said, "I will dwell in them, and I will be their God, and they shall be My people. Wherefore **come out** from among them, and be separate," says the Lord, "and **touch not** the unclean thing; and I will receive you, and will be a Father unto you, and you shall be My sons and daughters," says the Lord Almighty. Having therefore these promises, dearly beloved, let us **cleanse ourselves** from all filthiness of the flesh and of the spirit, perfecting holiness in the fear of God* (II Corinthians 6:14-7:1).

Are you a part of a "Church, Inc." – a governmentally formed and controlled religious entity? Are you a part of a 501c3 organization, officially approved, recognized and sanctioned by the federal government?

If so, then you are fellow religious members with every *"unclean thing"* (II Corinthians 6:17), and I encourage you, as we are entreated by Paul, to *"come out from among them,"* that we *"touch not the unclean thing,"* and that we *"cleanse ourselves from all filthiness of the flesh and spirit ..."* (II Corinthians 7:1).

According to the context, all of this *"unclean"* stuff is the Gentile religious system.

Do you think that *"your* church" or *"your* ministry" is not a part of this system, that you are not a member together with them? If you don't think that you are, then call the bank where your "church" or "ministry" does business. They will tell you what you are! They can also tell you under what Federal "class" you are categorized. They could also tell you who else is in that "class" with you.

Or ask the Federal Government – the IRS in particular. They know what you are. They know what group and class you belong to. You may try to deny what you are, but you are in with all the rest of the religions – Muslim, Buddhist, Wiccan, Satanist, CHRISTIAN; as far as this nation is concerned, you're *all* the same!

It is all really simple. The world knows what we are, even if we try to pretend that we are really different. We are self-deceived. I say *we*, because I have been where you are. I was a part of something that has a religious legal identity, one that I pretended didn't really exist, and one that, on occasion, I will even speak against – but I was a part of it just the same! I encourage you to be honest with yourself and with the world around you. Come clean.

> *Therefore seeing we have this ministry, as we have received mercy, we faint not; but have **renounced the hidden things of dishonesty, not walking in craftiness, nor handling the Word of God deceitfully;** but by manifestation of the truth commending ourselves to every man's conscience in the sight of God* (II Corinthians 4:1-2).

Stop trying to pawn off *your* "church" as the *"church of God."* Stop joining forces with the religious systems of this world! I encourage you to leave the system. Come on outside the camp!

WOULD PAUL HAVE QUALIFIED FOR "501C3" STATUS?

The following is taken directly from the IRS code:

IRC 501(c)(3) – Religious Purposes

Churches are a subset of IRC 501(c)(3) organizations organized and operated for religious purposes. See, e.g., De La Salle Institute v. United States, 195 F. Supp. 891 (N.D. Cal. 1961); Chapman v. Commissioner, 43 T.C. 358, 363 (1967).

501(c)(3) Requirements

An organization must be described in IRC 501(c)(3) to qualify as a church under IRC 170(b)(1)(A)(i), although it need not be recognized as such by the Service (given that churches are exempt from the filing requirements of IRC 508(a) and (b)).

In determining if a religious organization is a church within the meaning of IRC 170(b)(1)(a)(i), 508(c)(1)(A), or 6033(a)(2)(A), consider if the organization has the following characteristics:

A distinct legal existence;
A recognized creed and form of worship;
A definite and distinct *ecclesia*stical government;
A formal code of doctrine and discipline;
A distinct religious history;
A membership not associated with any other church or denomination;
A complete organization of ordained ministers ministering to their congregations;
Ordained ministers selected after completing prescribed courses of study;
A literature of its own;
Established place of worship;
Regular congregations;
Regular religious services;
Sunday schools for the religious instruction of the young;

Schools for the preparation of its ministers; and

Any other facts and circumstances that may bear upon the organization's claim for church status.

Now, we have one simple question: Would Paul have qualified?

If not, then how is it that we can follow him, and yet we can qualify for this religious, governmentally sanctioned distinction?

Pressing the Issue

In Paul's day, Israel's religion had long been a part of the Roman religious system. It was a legitimately recognized religion by the government. It was *religio licita* (had official religious license) from Rome.

Did it ever occur to you why Paul, a Roman born citizen, had legal battles and ended up executed by Rome?

When Paul started his ministry he was undoubtedly recognized under the *religio licita* of Judaism; but he received progressive *"revelations"* (II Corinthians 12:1) from the Lord concerning *"the mystery"* (Ephesians 3:3). The more truth he received and taught, the more he distanced himself and the *ecclesia* from Israel. The more clearly and strongly he taught, *"rightly dividing the Word of Truth"* (II Timothy 3:15), the more he was saying in essence, "This is not that," "the church the Body of Christ is not Israel." From town to town, and speech by speech, he was pounding nails in his own coffin. He was identifying the church, the Body of Christ as being outside of the religious system. He operated *religio illicita* (as an illegal, unlicensed religion); but this was his intent, for which he would lay down his life!

He builds too low who builds beneath the skies. (Anon.)

Paul gives us a solemn warning:

... *Let every man take heed how he builds* ... (I Corinthians 3:10).

INSTITUTIONALIZATION OF GOD

Our culture has developed a system of dealing with our aged parents and grandparents. We "put them away" in institutions for the elderly. It is all neat and clean. They are out of our daily lives and we can go about our daily business and lives, going to visit them on weekends, schedules permitting.

The sad thing is that we have done this in our minds with God for a long time. God is neatly tucked away from our daily lives. His worship and service are even tucked away, because we do that on Sunday at the "worship service"!

- Where does God *dwell?*
- Where do you *worship* God?
- Where do you *serve* God?
- Where does *ministry* take place in your life?

Have you limited these activities to some man-made *institution?* Most of the Body of Christ has. This is sad beyond description! Shame on us! Will we continue to be party to such a conspiracy against God? A conspiracy it is: It is a conspiracy against the truth of His Word, the truth of our identity, the truth of His very Own character and attributes. Resist this "institutionalization of God"! Refuse to allow our God to be "put away"!

Protest by refusing to participate in such a practice any longer! Let us be free to be who we are! **We** are the church, **we** are the house of God, **we** are the habitation of God, **we** are His building. The worship, service and ministry of God are daily features of His life in us and are not regulated by time or place. Let's stand *there!*

> *I am crucified with Christ: nevertheless I live; yet not I, but* **Christ lives in me:** *and the life that I now live in the flesh* **I live by the faith of the Son of God,** *Who loved me, and gave Himself for me* (Galatians 2:20).

THE DANGER OF THE "HOUSE CHURCH" MOVEMENT: RELIGIOUS TRADITION IN DISGUISE

When Paul uses the phrase, *"the church in your house,"* he is not referring to the building or architectural "house." Instead he is referring to the "household" (*i.e.*, the family itself). The Greek word that Paul uses for *"house"* is *oikos* (house, usually the household) instead of *oikia* (house, usually the building).

> The most common words to express the concept of family in the New Testament are *oikos*, *"house,"* and its derivatives. *Oikos* may indicate the couple, their children, and any servants or relatives living in the house (I Timothy 3:5, 12). – Lawrence O. Richards, *Zondervan Expository Dictionary of Bible Words*

> *Oikos* ... by implication, a family. – James Strong, *Strong's Greek Lexicon, #3624, Strong's Exhaustive Concordance*

> *Oikos* ... by metonymy, of the members of a household or family. – W.E. Vine, *Vine's Expository Dictionary of New Testament Words*

There is a growing movement afloat called "the House Church Movement." It has, in some circles and areas, become quite popular. It's an acceptable, alternative "thing to do." Home is where the "members" of this movement **"do** church."

I would like to be clear that this is not what Paul is talking about when he utilized the phrase *"the church in your house."* He was not talking about a *house church movement.* Paul was not a part of *any* man-made movement. The only movement he knew anything about was the natural movement of Christ through the members of His Body.

This should be a good enough "movement" for us: Christ living and moving through the members of His Body. This should be the only movement of which we would desire to be a part!

Why is it that members of Christ's Body seem never to be satisfied with their identity in Christ? Why is it that we have this pressing desire to be recognized and identified with something else – *anything else* – beyond Christ?

House Church and Home Church?

Now, the fact is that there is no such term in Scripture as "house church" or "home church," anymore than there is the term "local church." Surely there will be those who will accuse us of "squabbling over semantics," but words *are* important – they mean things. There is a vast difference between "the local church" and *the church* in a locality; and just the same, there is a vast difference between "the house church" or "the home church," and **"the church** in your house."

The church is not something we "do," it is not somewhere we "go." It is who we *are!* We *are* the church whether we are at work, at school, or on vacation. Yet we do not use the terms "work church," "school church," or "vacation church" to describe these. We are simply *the church* at work, *the church* at school, *the church* on vacation.

The church is everywhere the saints are! It is everywhere its members (*i.e.*, Body parts) are, and when *the church* gathers it is not "doing" church, it is not "going" to church. We were *the church* before we gather, we are *the church* when we gather, and we are *the church* when we disassemble! Anchor this truth in your soul: WE **ARE** THE CHURCH!

That's why the Scriptures tell us that Paul *"gathered the church together"* (Acts 14:27). What was Paul gathering? Bricks and mortar? No! An organization? No! He was gathering *the church*. He was gathering *saints*. He was gathering Body parts, and they were *the church*, even when they were not meeting. So, neither is the meeting *the church!*

Do you begin to see the problem with "house church," and "home church?" It brings us right back to the exact same problem that the traditional "church" has. It steals *our* identity. "House church" and "home church" are not God's church! They are man's pitiful attempts at imitation!

Now, we appreciate what some in the "House Church Movement" have done to awaken many to the problems with the traditional "church"; but, to some degree, the "House Church Movement" has replaced one architectural form (the chapel) with another (the house). The danger is that we carry the system of the chapel into the home. Have we simply swapped "having church" in a chapel with "having church" in a house? If so, the primary difference is architecture, and architecture is *not* even close to being the issue!

The issue is the life of Christ living in and through *His church* – when, where and how He pleases! Every day, in every place, and within *every* circumstance – Christ is manifesting Himself in His living church! **This** is *"the house of God!"* **This** is *"the church of the living God!"* **This** is *"the pillar and ground of the truth!"* **This** is *"the mystery of godliness!"*

> But if I tarry long, that you may know how you ought to behave yourself in the house of God, which is the church of the living God, the pillar and ground of the truth. And without controversy great is the mystery of godliness … (I Timothy 3:15-16).

"The church in your house" supports these truths. The "house church" and "home church" supplant them! (It's religious tradition under **guise** of Bible truth.)

Are you *the church*, or do you "do church?" Do you "go to" a "house church?"

Don't settle for *anything* less than who and what God has made you in Christ!

OFFERING TO GOD WHAT HE DOES NOT WANT

For you see your calling, brothers, how that not many wise men after the flesh, not many mighty, not many noble, are called: but God has chosen the foolish things of the world to confound the wise; and God has chosen the weak things of the world to confound the things which are mighty; and the base things of the world, and the things which are despised, has God chosen, yea, and the things which are not, to bring to nought the things that are: that no flesh should glory in His presence. But of Him are you in Christ Jesus, Who of God is made unto us wisdom, and righteousness, and sanctification, and redemption: that, according as it is written, "He who glories, let him glory in the Lord" (I Corinthians 1:26-31).

God has chosen to use the foolish, weak, base and despised things of this world to bring about His Own purpose and glory. Yet, how often do we as believers, following the course of this world, seek to offer to God what He does not want? We seek to offer Him something impressive, something mighty, something lofty, something logical, something noble, and something BIG.

Our dreams are to give God something worthy of His greatness, but in so doing we undermine His very purpose. As sincere as our motives may be, they are human, not divine. We have missed the divine viewpoint, and seek to elevate our own wisdom, strength and ingenuity above His. We are like Cain, bringing God an offering of our own choosing – offering God something from our own hands.

The world looks for greatness, prestige, prominence, honor and reputation. We must abandon our earthly perspectives and recognize that God looks for foolish, weak, base and despised things. We can ultimately rejoice in this, because we have *exactly* what God is looking for! As we submit to this divine plan, we can be used to give God what He wants, and in the process bring Him, and Him alone, glory!

Let's give up our large and noble ambitions!

Let's stop offering God what He does not want!

THE RELIGIOUS SYSTEM

Except the LORD builds the house, they labor in vain who build it (Psalms 127:1).

Are we still following the religious course of this world? Man has taken the entire dispensation of grace – up until our day – to demonstrate clearly that all human religious institutions, no matter how humbly and focused they seem to begin, end up in apostasy. What is it that makes us feel that we can do better? Are we smarter? Are we more spiritual? What do we have that others have not had?

There is something about the very nature of religious organizations that eventually shifts the focus off of the original message, ministry and spirit of its purpose, and transfers it to themselves. They take on a life of their own. All of them eventually do. Some of them do it more quickly than others. Some take a generation or two.

Do we dare to attempt success in a human concept that has managed *only* to demonstrate failure? Shall we create a future *monster* to deliver to our children and grandchildren? Is concern over preserving finances, maintaining some type of religious "testimony," or whatever our goal may be, really worth the *risk,* even if it were *only* a small one? Shall we leave our children with religious politicking and power struggles, with misplaced direction and love, with endless business meetings, financial statements and squabbles, with their attention and focus off of personal relationships and ministry and on the perpetuation and control of "the institution"?

To emphasize the point, let's look at a quote from *The Berean Searchlight,* May, 1996 (all emphasis in this quote is as it appeared in the publication):

Paul warns us about those who, whether wittingly or unwittingly, would spread unsound doctrine among us. We are living in a time when some of the brethren seem to deem it important to find something new. Of course, it is not our intent to discourage anyone in regard to exercising the "Berean spirit." However, care should be taken not to undermine the *foundation* upon which our faith rests. We do well to remember that "The Doctrinal Statement" our forefathers forged for us was a product of intense debate with the denominational leaders of their day. Each plank of the statement was carefully crafted as a *defense* and *confirmation* of the Fundamentals of the faith and Paul's gospel. Therefore, let us not be too quick to challenge those things which are "tried and true." ... Our "Doctrinal Statement," ... has served us well for over fifty years ...

Does such a statement trouble you?

Is "the foundation" upon which your faith rests "The Doctrinal Statement"? This is a sad commentary on organized religion.

PAUL THE TENTMAKER

Paul, our apostle (Romans 11:13), made his living as a tentmaker (Acts 18:3). He conducted his life and ministry outside of the religious system. He taught the divine value and purpose of work.

Many believe that to *really* serve God, one must be religiously "employed," but the truth of the matter is that every believer is called to "full time" ministry in the context of their individual daily lives (I Corinthians 10:31; II Corinthians 5:18).

"Tentmaking" will find its own unique form in how we make a living. We may be a construction worker, or a computer technician. We may farm, or do electrical work. Perhaps we are a physician, salesman, or teacher. It matters little in the eternal perspective of things what the details of our "tentmaking" involves. The important thing is that we are "tentmaking."

No matter what the circumstances of life are around us are, regardless of what earthly occupation we may use to supply our needs and those of others, we each have a divine vocation to which we have been called. Yet it is not "tentmaking" that defines us or our lives. Paul was not *"Paul, the tentmaker."* No, he was defined by heaven in light of his divine calling and vocation; he was *"Paul, the apostle."*

We live our lives for the Lord, serving Him, and we do so in the context of "tentmaking." More often than not, this context can have the appearance of a monotonous, daily routine; but the very Life of God running its full course in our day-by-day circumstances will make our lives anything but monotonous and routine.

We must not confuse what we do to make a living with the purpose of our lives. Our occupations are just the contexts in which we carry out our divine calling. The circumstances of our earthly labors are the backdrop of God's working in our lives.

For we are His workmanship, created in Christ Jesus unto good works, which God has before ordained that we should walk in them (Ephesians 2:10).

RELIGIOUS HIRELINGS

He who is an hireling, and not the shepherd, whose own the sheep are not, sees the wolf coming, and leaves the sheep, and flees: and the wolf catches them, and scatters the sheep. The hireling flees, because he is an hireling, and cares not for the sheep (John 10:12-13).

Noah Webster defines "hireling" as "one who is hired, or who serves for wages." Truly, *religious* hirelings are the respected order of the day.

As believers, we are to regard our *"secular"* employment as divine – *"as unto the Lord"* (Ephesians 6:5-8; Colossians 3:22-24; Titus 2:9-10). Thus, each believer's vocation is indeed a high calling of God (Ephesians 4:1). As William Carey (1761-1834) would say, "My business is preaching the gospel, and I cobble shoes to pay my expenses."

It is amazing how the tables have turned. Often the man who teaches God's Word is disdained if he is not *religiously* "salaried," as if he were not genuine. The fact is that Paul was not for "hire." Rather, he was the bond-slave of Jesus Christ, making his living as a humble laborer – a *"tentmaker"* (Acts 18:1-3).

Witness Lee brings his own testimony:

> Paul worked with his hands at making tents (Acts 18:3) in order to support both himself and those who were with him. He worked in order to help his young co-workers. This indicates that Paul's way was not that of today's clergy who make a profession out of preaching.[12]

---

12. Witness Lee, *Life-Study of Acts*, p. 479.

NUMBERING PEOPLE: A GENTILE OBSESSION

We have an inherent obsession with numbering people. We are impressed by it. It is a vexation of our spirit that carries over into our view of spiritual life. We assume that if it is of God, or for God, it must be large and involve many people.

Listen to what people say:

> How many believe what you believe?
> How many do you have on Sunday?
> How many were at the Conference?
> How many are attending Bible study now?
> How many are on your mailing list?
> How many …?

Just pay attention next time you are with other Christians. You might be amazed at how *central* this concept is thought to be in our "spiritual" life.

However God is not so obsessed and impressed. He is not bound or motivated by such a Gentile viewpoint.

Let's reflect on a few Biblical examples.

Noah and the Ark

> *And spared not the old world, but saved Noah the eighth person, a preacher of righteousness, bringing in the flood upon the world of the ungodly* (II Peter 2:5).

> *Which sometime were disobedient, when once the longsuffering of God waited in the days of Noah, while the ark was a preparing, wherein few, that is, eight souls were saved by water* (I Peter 3:20).

God's work in the ark resulted in the world-wide saving of eight souls. Count them – eight souls. This is not very impressive by Gentile standards (nor Christendom's either!).

Gideon's 300

Israel was facing the Midianites in battle, who, with the Amalekites were situated,

> Along in the valley like grasshoppers for a multitude; and their camels were without number, as the sand by the sea side for a multitude (Judges 7:1).

Gideon had one small problem: he "only" had 32,000 men to fight against them. God, however, had a different view: He thought that Gideon had *too many* in his army.

> The people that are with you are too many for Me to give the Midianites into their hands, lest Israel vaunt themselves against Me, saying, "My own hand has saved me" (Judges 7:2).

So God had Gideon reduce the number. He told Gideon to tell the people, "*Whosoever is fearful and afraid, let him return and depart ...*" (:3). The result? 22,000 departed. Gideon's army was reduced to 10,000 men. Yet God said that there were *still* "too many" (:4), so He gave them a test that resulted in the release of another 9,700 men. Gideon was then left with an army of 300.

God used Gideon and his army of 300 to do the job against "*a multitude*"!

The 3,000 and 5,000 in Acts

The Book of Acts is sometimes viewed as a place where positive significance is given to "large" numbers:

> Then they who gladly received His word were baptized: and the same day there were added unto them about three thousand souls (Acts 2:41).

> Howbeit many of them who heard the word believed; and the number of the men was about five thousand (Acts 4:4).

This all sounds very impressive doesn't it? Yet these two numberings are really a part of the indictment against Israel. Think about it for a moment: God had been dealing with Israel (Abraham's physical descendants) for over two millennia. He had sent them a host of prophets; He had given them His Word; He had sent them His Son; and what was the national result? 5,000 men! *5,000* men from an entire nation? **5,000** *men from an entire nation after over 2,000 years of work!?* This would seem more like an indictment against the Nation. So maybe we need to adjust our Gentile thinking to match the context – maybe these numbers are not as impressive as they may first appear.

The Garden of Eden

The ultimate illustration may be at the very beginning. In Eden's garden, how many people did God make? He made one man and one woman. Now, think about that for a moment – He could have made multiple men and women. In so doing he could have provided other women for Eve with whom to do "girl things." He could have provided a wonderful opportunity in the garden for "women's fellowship and Bible study meetings" – but this was not in the mind of God.

In making multiple men, God also could have provided Adam with other men with whom to do "guy things." They could have had "men's meetings," and they could have had a sympathetic ear as they shared things that they could not talk about with their wives (what things?) – yet, neither was this in the mind of God.

Then, of course, in making multiple men and women, God could have provided other couples for Adam and Eve with whom to "hang out" and do "group" things together. These multiple couples could have also provided children for Cain and Able with whom to socialize. They could have played together, and even have been assembled together for social and educational purposes – but neither was this necessary in the mind of God.

God Is Interested in Weighing People

As we study the Scriptures, one thing which we will learn is that God is not so concerned with counting people, but in weighing them:

> *You are weighed in the balances, and are found wanting* (Daniel 5:27).

The issue with God is one of personal faithfulness:

> *Moreover it is required in stewards, that a man is found faithful* (I Corinthians 4:2).

> *... The same commit to faithful men, who shall be able to teach others also* (II Timothy 2:2).

Sort, Not Size

God is looking not for *size*, but a certain *sort* of work!

> *... The fire shall try every man's work of what sort it is* (I Corinthians 3:13).

THE FEW OF PAUL'S MINISTRY

In the early part of the book of Acts we read of the 3,000 and then of the 5,000. While reading on in the book of Acts, when we come to Paul and His Gentile ministry, we don't read of specific numbers like this. How many were actually involved in Paul's ministry? What do you usually visualize when you think of his work?

Let's take the capital of the Roman Empire for example. How many believers were at Rome when Paul wrote to them? It would appear from Romans chapter 16 that there were as many as five households represented there (*"the church in your house"*). Now, how many saints could be connected with a specific household (family members, servants, friends, etc.)? Perhaps 10 to 30? These numbers multiplied by 5 household would be a total range from 50 to 150. This number would not just be men (as are the 5,000 numbered in the book of Acts), but men, women and children in 5 home gatherings in the capital of the Roman Empire. This was after some 15 years of Pauline ministry in the Empire. Impressive? It depends on one's viewpoint; but the story grows more interesting!

Paul actually went to Rome and taught for two years. During Paul's first Roman imprisonment he served under house arrest. This worked out to a great advantage for Paul, for we read in the Book of Acts,

> *And Paul dwelled two whole years in his own hired house, and received all who came in unto him, preaching the kingdom of God, and teaching those things which concern the Lord Jesus Christ, with all confidence, no man forbidding him* (Acts 28:30-31).

You would think after this two-year teaching ministry of Paul, out of his own rented house, that we might see a great influx in numbers. Yet the truth is that it got worse!

Paul wrote the Book of II Timothy from Rome, but when he writes Timothy this last time, what does he say?

All they who are in Asia are turned away from me (II Timothy 1:15).

Paul addresses the Asian problem because this was where Timothy was. This is the ruins of which Timothy was personally aware. That's why he starts that statement,

This you know, that all they who are in Asia are turned away from me.

If the truth be known, this apostasy of the Body of Christ proliferated throughout the entire Roman Empire. While in this last Roman imprisonment Paul said, concerning his first trial date,

No man stood with me, but all men forsook me (II Timothy 4:16).

There was not one man in Rome who came and stood with Paul! This was after some 23 years of ministry in the Roman Empire. It was after writing an epistle to the saints at Rome, and it was after coming to Rome and having a two-year house teaching ministry there. What happened to the Roman saints? Now we can't even count 5 households.

A "NOT MANY" MINISTRY

Paul's was a *"not many"* ministry, and so it is with ours. The *"not many"* ministry is the ministry to which God has called us!

> *For you see your calling, brothers, how that not many wise men after the flesh, not many mighty, not many noble, are called* (I Corinthians 1:26).

When we ask Paul, "How many ...?" Paul gives us the answer: *"Not many!"* So, the next time you are asked one of those "How many" questions, simply reply, "Not many!"

Instead of a "many" ministry, ours is a *"foolish," "weak," "base," "despised,"* and *"things that are not"* – i.e., "nothing" – ministry!

> *For you see your calling, brothers, how that not many wise men after the flesh, not many mighty, not many noble, are called: but God has chosen the foolish things of the world to confound the wise; and God has chosen the weak things of the world to confound the things which are mighty; and the base things of the world, and the things which are despised, has God chosen, yea, and the things which are not, to bring to nought the things that are: that no flesh should glory in His presence. But of Him are you in Christ Jesus, Who of God is made unto us wisdom, and righteousness, and sanctification, and redemption: that, according as it is written, "He who glories, let him glory in the Lord"* (I Corinthians 1:26-31).

Let's not allow ourselves to be carried away with the Gentile obsession of numbering people. Let's not fight the divine plan and viewpoint! Let's stop contending with God.

THE OFF-SCOURING

In contrast to the religious system, which secures acceptability, honor, prestige and respectability before the community and the world, Paul was viewed as the *"off-scouring of all things."*

> *Being defamed, we entreat: we are made as the filth of the world, and are the off-scouring of all things unto this day* (I Corinthians 4:13).

Paul was viewed as "filth" and "off-scouring"! Let's look at these words briefly:

Filth – James Strong[13] defines this word as "refuse." Noah Webster[14] defines it as, "Dirt; any foul matter; any thing that soils or defiles; waste matter; nastiness."

Off-scouring – now, there is an interesting word. Strong defines it as "off-scrapings (fig., scum)." Webster defines it as, "That which is scoured off; hence, refuse; rejected matter; that which is vile or despised."

Every time I think of this passage and Paul's use of the word "off-scouring," I am reminded of the kitchen sink. When I grew up, my mother mainly used iron pans in her cooking. After something extra good had been fired-up in the iron skillet, inevitably the time came for cleanup. The iron skillet was placed down into a pan of clean water and a scouring pad was applied. When the job was complete, nothing else could be washed in *that* water! In fact it was *good-for-nothing* water. It was one of the nastiest sinks of water one would ever want to see. It was filled with *off-scouring*. Anybody thirsty? Of course not! This is disgusting.

That was the world view of Paul. He was "scum." If we are seeking to be recognized and accepted by the world, we will have to follow another course other than Paul's.

---

13. James Strong, *Strongs Exhaustive Concordance.*
14. Noah Webster, *American Dictionary of the English Language,* 1828.

Instead of bearing the simple names of who we are *in Christ*, such as saint or brother, leaders of religious movements would prefer titles that would be more acceptable to the world – titles that would identify who they are *in the system,* such as "Reverend," "Doctor," "Founder," "Director," "President," etc. How impressive they all sound! They seem to make us *something* before the eyes of the world, and give some type of legitimate *standing;* but are we not already something, and do we not already have a standing? Why would we want to have something more than what we already have in Christ?

BELONGING

Most of us have a built-in desire to "fit in." We have a deep-seated longing to "belong" – and not just to anything – but to belong to something significant, something respectable, something *big!*

However, the fact is, we *already* belong to something! Something that is not of *this* world. Something that is apart from the religious and world systems. It is something that is eternal and heavenly – it is the church, the Body of Christ.

As we have already seen, from the world view, God has chosen things that are foolish, weak, base and despised. So we must always keep in mind that there are two conflicting viewpoints. Let's not allow ourselves to be pressured by the religious and world systems. Let's not be pressured into abandoning God's assessment of things. Let's not be drawn into the world's mutual admiration societies!

High Esteem

In His ministry to Israel while on earth, the Lord Jesus Christ pointed out a profound and significant truth:

> *You are they who justify yourselves before men; but God knows your hearts: for that which is highly esteemed among men is an abomination in the sight of God* (Luke 16:15).

We would do well to ponder this in our hearts.

True Success

Sometimes it is hard for us to estimate real value. The problem occurs because there are two viewpoints: the human and the divine. How do we measure real success? All true success will be determined at the Judgment Seat of Christ!

> *For we must all appear before the Judgment Seat of Christ; that every one may receive the things done in his body, according*

to that he has done, whether it is good or bad (II Corinthians 5:10).

On the other side of this life things will not appear as they do here.

Moreover it is required in stewards that a man be found faithful. But with me it is a very small thing that I should be judged of you, or of man's judgment: yea, I judge not my own self. For I know nothing by myself; yet am I not hereby justified: but He Who judges me is the Lord. Therefore judge nothing before the time, until the Lord comes, Who both will bring to light the hidden things of darkness, and will make manifest the counsels of the hearts, and then shall every man have praise of God (I Corinthians 4:2-5).

If all of this is true (and it is!), then we should live our lives with a celestial view. It is only through this view – the divine viewpoint – that we are able to build that which has true success.

While we look not at the things which are seen, but the things which are not seen: for the things which are seen are temporal; but the things which are not seen are eternal (II Corinthians 4:18).

STOLEN IDENTITY

I was glad when they said unto me, "Let us go into the house of the Lord" (Psalm 122:1).

One of the fastest growing crimes in our day is identity theft. Larger and larger numbers are finding that their identity has been assumed by others. With this stolen identity professional thieves have been able to amass great wealth by fraud. Yet identity theft is nothing new for the church, the Body of Christ. Our true identity has been stolen from us. That's right: human organizations and institutions, along with their brick and mortar structures, have assumed for themselves *our* identity *"in Christ."*

The "Reformation" never did free the members of Christ's Body from this type of religious fraud; and centuries later, in spite of all of the truth to which the Body of Christ has been exposed, it is still common practice to simply surrender our true identity to the religious system:

- "Remember that this is the Lord's House."
- "Welcome to the House of God."
- "Be reverent when entering the sanctuary."

Now, there was a time when these three phrases would have had legitimate meaning – for example Psalm 122:1, *"I was glad when they said unto me, 'Let us go into the house of the Lord'"* – but to what was this passage referring, and to whom was this written?

First of all, we must realize that at the time this was written the Body of Christ did not, as yet, exist. If we *rightly divide the Word of Truth* (in accordance with II Timothy 2:15), we can understand that the audience of that particular Scripture was Israel, and it was a reference to a physical structure.

In time past, Israel had the Temple. It was God's House in that day (*c.f.* II Chronicles 7:1-2, 5). It was the meeting place of God with Israel; but today, in the dispensation of grace, we – the members of

Christ's Body – are God's house.

Yet how often have we heard Psalm 122:1 – *"I was glad when they said unto me, 'Let us go into the house of the Lord'"* – used in reference to some man-made structure in the dispensation of grace? This takes the passage out of its dispensational context. It is an illegitimate use of the passage. The truth of the matter is that any physical building presented as "the house of the Lord" today is a fraud. *We* are the church. *We* are the house of God. God lives *in us – we're* His church building!

On an even sadder note, we have been party to all of this identity fraud. We have supported and helped build such a system – with our presence and with our money – and all the while it was taking our identity from us, and using it for ill-gotten gain!

When will we wake up and realize that our identity has been taken from us? When will we understand that we have ever been aiding and abetting the Adversary in this serious crime? When will we reclaim our true identity and live in the fullness of who and what we are *in Christ?*

It is high time that this evil crime against the Body of Christ be reported. Let's search the Scriptures and learn of our true identity as God's church, God's house. Then let's report these truths to the saints. Let's ask them if they know that there are those out there parading under the pretense of being us. Let's encourage others to reclaim their identity and expose this scam.

ONE CHURCH – ONE BODY – ONE MEMBERSHIP,

or,

TWO CHURCHES – TWO BODIES – TWO MEMBERSHIPS

One of the lines above represents the truth of the dispensation of grace. The other represents the methods of man. Many believers claim membership in two churches. They are professing membership in two bodies.

A man will be a member of the First Community Church, for example, while also claiming membership in *the church,* which is His Body. This man holds membership in two "bodies." Thus he professes two churches, two bodies, and two memberships; but in reality, by practice, he is denying the ONE church, the ONE Body, and the ONE membership (Colossians 1:18).

Be and enjoy who and what you are in Christ!

Help lead others to this wonderful place!

DENOMINATIONALISM

... Let us make us a name ... (Genesis 11:4).

The Body of Christ has long been plagued by the sectarian spirit and the divisiveness of denominationalism. Webster, in his 1828 *American Dictionary of the English Language*, defines *denomination* as:

> The act of naming ... A class, society or collection of individuals, called by the same name; as a *denomination* of Christians.

Denomination comes from the word *denominate,* which is defined by Webster as:

> To name, to give a name or epithet to ...

During the current dispensation, God is using the glorious gospel of grace to call out a people unto Himself. They are placed into living union with His Son. God has given this organism a name: the church, the Body of Christ.

Throughout the dispensation of grace, many members of Christ's Body have failed to understand and appreciate *fully* their Divine completeness in Christ (Colossians 2:10). They have therefore become dissatisfied with being what and whom God made them in Christ. They have sought to establish their *own* institutions and have given them names of their *own* choosing.

Such human enterprises have often found *acceptability, honor, prestige* and *respectability* before the world. Yet the question we should ask is, "Does it bring glory to God to rival His organism and name with an organization and name of our own?" Is it not the SON, and the Body that is identified with Him, that bring glory to the Father?

Paul wrote:

> *But God forbid that I should glory, save in the cross of our Lord*

Jesus Christ, by Whom the world is crucified unto me, and I unto the world (Galatians 6:14).

When asked, "To what church do you belong?" or "Where are you a member?" why do we feel *inadequate* with simply being members of Christ's Body? Why do we feel the need to go beyond what God has done? Are we *ashamed* of being identified only with what He has done, and is doing with the church, the Body of Christ?

But I fear, lest by any means, as the serpent beguiled Eve through subtlety, so your minds should be corrupted from the simplicity that is in Christ (II Corinthians 11:3).

THE PERSONAL NATURE OF BIBLE STUDY

The study of the Scriptures ("Bible study") is an extremely personal matter. Paul told Timothy, *"Study to show yourself approved."* He was not here advocating group, but personal Bible study.

Sometimes believers will gather together for what they call "Bible Study." The whole concept of "Bible Study" as a meeting is as foreign to the Scriptures as having "Worship" as a meeting. "Bible Study" as a meeting is a man-made religious invention to divert from the real study of Scripture, just as "Worship" as a meeting diverts from true worship.

There are only three occurrences of the word "study" in the Bible, two of which are Paul's. These two instructions to study could not possibly be any more personal or private in nature:

> *Study to show yourself approved unto God, a workman who needs not to be ashamed, rightly dividing the Word of Truth* (II Timothy 2:15).

> *And that you study to be quiet, and to do your own business, and to work with your own hands, as we commanded you* (I Thessalonians 4:11).

The divine purpose of the gathering of believers was never designed to be centered on what we commonly refer to as "Bible Study." The study of the Scriptures is not an occasional group activity. It is an extremely personal thing. We each have a responsibility to become acquainted with the Scriptures on a personal level, instead of hiding in a sea of faces at a "Bible Study." Even those Bereans who gathered to hear Paul, the Apostle to the Gentiles, the divinely appointed spokesman for the Body of Christ, would *"prove all things"* by *"searching the Scriptures daily, whether those things were so."*

This is what set the Bereans apart as noble:

These [those of Berea] *were more noble than those in Thessalonica, in that they received the Word with all readiness of mind, and searched the Scriptures daily, whether those things were so* (Acts 17:11).

Appendix I

Habitat for Divinity

We are going to take a look at the *dwelling place* of God. We will briefly be working our way through the chronology of the Bible to see where on earth God is. These insights will lead us to a most amazing truth – God's great truth for today – so let's get started. We will begin *"In the beginning ..."*

> And they heard the voice of the Lord God walking in the garden in the cool of the day ... (Genesis 3:8).

Think of it! Adam lived in a beautiful garden located in a place called Eden, which means *pleasure*. It was a place of breathless wonder. He lived there with a counterpart prepared especially for him by his Creator, but more importantly GOD was with him in the garden!

Take that in. Can you even imagine that? Adam lived in a garden of *pleasure* and GOD was there; God was walking on the planet. God was in Adam's "neck of the woods." Could we find adequate words to describe such a wonderfully blessed situation?

Nevertheless, with one action there was a "disastrous" *turn of events*. Adam and Eve sinned against God their Creator. The very next portion of this passage reads:

> And Adam and his wife hid themselves from the presence of the Lord God amongst the trees of the garden (3:8).

The presence of God was on the Earth and Adam and Eve *"hid themselves"* from Him. Sadly the presence of the Lord God had become a *fearful* thing. How "disastrous" sin is – how fearful and alienating!

And the Lord God called unto Adam, and said unto him, "Where are you?" And he said, "I heard Your voice in the garden, and I was afraid, because I was naked; and I hid myself" (3:9).

The end result of this sad account is that God,

... drove out the man; and He placed at the east of the garden of Eden Cherubims, and a flaming sword which turned every way, to keep the way of the Tree of Life (3:24).

Life in *the presence* of God was over!

GOD'S DWELLING IN THE TABERNACLE AND TEMPLE

And let them make Me a sanctuary: that I may dwell among them (Exodus 25:8).

Many years after the fall, God came to *dwell among* man once again. He came to live among His chosen nation, Israel. He instructed them to build a dwelling place for Him, which was called the *tabernacle* in its temporary form, and the *temple* in its more permanent version (I Kings 8:12-13). The tabernacle and temple were distinctly known as *"the house of the Lord," "the Lord's house," "the house of God"* (II Chronicles 7:1-2, 5), because that's where God dwelled. It was His *"sanctuary"* from the world that was at enmity with Him.

Imagine it! The children of Israel had the *True* and *Living* God, the God of the universe as one of their national residents, one of their neighbors. They were able to boast that God dwelled among them! When folks visited Jerusalem, they could be taken over by *God's house* to see where the Eternal God lived. What a wonder! Can you imagine that? Could any sightseeing attraction of the world rival that? God was in Israel's "neck of the woods." What a blessed circumstance!

However, once again, through a "disastrous" *turn of events* – the many spiritual whoredoms of the children of Israel – this house became *"Ich-*

abod ... the glory is departed from Israel" (I Samuel 4:21-22).

Life in *the presence* of God was over – again!

WHERE ON EARTH IS GOD?

When it comes to a study of the dwelling place of God, there comes an amazing turn of events when we get to Paul, the Apostle. By taking the important *dispensational* principles and *identification* truths which he revealed, we not only see WHO we are in Christ, but WHAT we are as well!

After the fall of Israel (Romans 11:11-12) God, through His chosen instrument Paul (Romans 11:13), turned to the Gentiles (Acts 13:46; 28:28). In so doing, God carried out His *mystery* plan which He had *"kept secret since the world began"* (Romans 16:25). The result of Christ's finished work at Calvary is that *"the riches of His grace"* are now manifested. We are thus *"accepted"* (Ephesians 1:6), *"complete"* (Colossians 2:10), and blessed with *"all spiritual blessings in heavenly places"* (Ephesians 1:3).

These wonderful truths are multifaceted. One of the many benefits of being *"in Christ,"* and there are many, is that we – those who were once *"without Christ, being aliens from the commonwealth of Israel, and strangers from the covenants of promise, having no hope, and without God in the world"* (Ephesians 2:12) – are *"now"* (2:13) *"a holy temple in the Lord"* (2:21), *"built together for an habitation of God through the Spirit"* (2:22).

None of us could have even imagined such an astounding turn of events: those who were strangers – without hope and without God – would become God's *dwelling place!*

Truly, what we have been given in His *"abundant grace"* is,

> ... *exceeding abundantly above all that we ask or think ...* (Ephesians 3:20).

He does more in *"the riches of His grace"* than we could ever *"ask or think."*

Honestly, we would never have dared to *"ask"* God for such an honor and privilege as having Him – the Sovereign of the Universe – actually live in us; nor would we ever have even been able to *"think"* up such a thing of magnificent grandeur.

"But the God of all grace" thought of it – and He did it!

We *are* now the *dwelling place* of God. It was His design, His choice, His doing; *"even a marvelous work and a wonder."*

HABITAT FOR DIVINITY

… You also are built together for an habitation of God … (Ephesians 2:22).

What a statement!

WE ARE THE TEMPLE, THE HABITATION OF GOD. Think of this! God not just dwelling in a building somewhere, but *in us!* That is truly something to get really excited about, I'd say!

There is an honorable movement in our country that builds homes for the underprivileged called *Habitat for Humanity;* but there is a far greater housing project underway today! It began some millennia ago. It is *Habitat for Divinity.* God is actively building a house for His own dwelling. A temple, *not* of bricks and mortar *made by hand,* but of people.

God Who made the world and all things therein, seeing that He is Lord of heaven and earth, dwells not in temples made with hands (Acts 17:24).

Know you not that you are the temple of God, and that the Spirit of God dwells in you? (I Corinthians 3:16).

What? Know you not that your body is the temple of the Holy Ghost which is in you, which you have of God, and you are not your own? (I Corinthians 6:19).

For you are the temple of the living God (II Corinthians 6:16).

In Whom all the building fitly framed together grows unto a holy temple in the Lord: in Whom you also are built together for a habitation of God through the Spirit (Ephesians 2:21-22).

Those of us who have now trusted Christ – the *first-trusters* – are the dwelling place of God! This is *much more* than walking with God in a garden; *much more* than having God as a neighbor; *much more* than having God in our "neck of the woods." We have the life of God IN US (*"manifest in the flesh"*)! He has taken up residence in us.

Habitat for Divinity; what a wonder!

What amazing grace!

OUR TRUE IDENTITY

Know you not that you are the temple of God, and that the Spirit of God dwells in you? (I Corinthians 3:16).

For most of us, our true identity as the *temple of God,* the *house of God,* has been stolen from us, years before we were ever born. Human organizations and institutions, along with their brick and mortar structures, have taken for themselves *our* identity *in Christ.* These religious agencies for too long have been pawned off as having the identity of the church, the Body of Christ.

Listen as many surrender their true identity:

"Where do you go to church?"
"Remember that this is the Lord's House."
"Welcome to the House of God."
"Be reverent when entering the sanctuary."

Identity Theft

Our identity has been stolen from us. It is reclaim our *true* identity and live in the fullness of who and what we are *"in Christ."* What does all this mean – to be the church, the temple, the sanctuary, the house of God? It means,

Living the Temple Life

The Old Testament will reveal the many aspects of *temple life*. Paul, our Apostle under grace, will show us how these aspects, once true of Israel's temple, are *now* true of us as members of Christ's Body.

Worship

Old Testament Temple: Psalm 5:7; Isaiah 66:23; Acts 7:48; Revelation 11:1

Grace Temple: Philippians 3:3

Singing

Old Testament Temple: Psalms 100:2; Amos 8:3

Grace Temple: Ephesians 5:19

Teaching

Old Testament Temple: Matthew 21:23

Grace Temple: II Timothy 2:15

Glory

Old Testament Temple: II Chronicles 7:1-2

Grace Temple: I Corinthians 2:6-7; II Corinthians 3:17-18; 4:6-7; Ephesians 3:19; Romans 8:18

Giving

Old Testament Temple: Malachi 3:10; Nehemiah 13:4-5

Grace Temple: I Corinthians 16:1

Sacrifice

Old Testament Temple: II Chronicles 7:4-5

Grace Temple: Romans 12:1-2; Philippians 2:17

Sweet Incense

Old Testament Temple: Exodus 30:7

Grace Temple: Ephesians 5:2

We have taken neither the time nor space to compare and contrast these points. Instead, they are given as an abridged concordance for our own personal study.

These truths should remind us that we are to *live* the temple life.

GOD MANIFEST IN THE FLESH

One God and Father of all, Who is above all, and through all, and in you all (Ephesians 4:6).

So, where on earth is God?

God is *in us!* The God of the universe lives in you and me. We are His dwelling place on earth today, and we take Him with us *everywhere* we go, making every act of ours an act of worship. What a blessed privilege that is. If folks are going to meet God, they are going to meet Him *in us.*

Jim Palmer wonderfully brought this truth to focus for us when he wrote,

> God is in our neighborhood because I carry His divine life within me. I put God ... in close proximity to others. With God in me, simply being present and available is "ministry." ...

> I've come to see the significance of my encounters with people as not pointing them *to* God as much as actually being an expression *of* God. The "Body of Christ" metaphor has grown in significance for me – that Christ continues His presence and ministry on earth in, through and as us ...

> God is not somewhere up in the sky; He's living His life in and through us, the Body of Christ, in the *neighborhoods where we live,* the places we work and play, and the people we come across each day. – *Wide Open Spaces* (2007), pages 34-35, 43

What a glorious mystery revealed to us by our Apostle, Paul; one that he calls, *"the great mystery;" "the mystery of godliness."*

> *This is a great mystery: but I speak concerning Christ and the church* (Ephesians 5:32).

> *To whom God would make known what is the riches of the glory of this mystery among the Gentiles; which is Christ in you, the hope of glory* (Colossians 1:27).

> *And without controversy great is the mystery of godliness: God was manifest in the flesh, justified in the Spirit, seen of angels, preached unto the Gentiles, believed on in the world, received up into glory* (I Timothy 3:16).

Godliness is not some moral or religious code followed; rather it is *"God manifest in the flesh."* God is the only meaning and definition of godliness. Christ is the only one who can live the godly life. We are God's dwelling place, and the Father seeks the manifestation of the life of His Son in our mortal flesh,

Always bearing about in the body the dying of the Lord Jesus, that the life also of Jesus might be made manifest in our body. For we who live are always delivered unto death for Jesus's sake, that the life also of Jesus might be made manifest in our mortal flesh (II Corinthians 4:10-11).

BEHAVE YOURSELF

But if I tarry long, that you may know how you ought to behave yourself in the house of God, which is the church of the living God, the pillar and ground of the truth. And without controversy great is the mystery of godliness: God was manifest in the flesh … (I Timothy 3:15-16).

We often hear parents tell their children to *"Behave!"* Yet the fact is that all children *behave*, though sometimes they just behave badly.

We may even hear religious parents say to their children, "Now I want you to behave yourself today in church." This is NOT the meaning of the verse above, *"behave yourself in the house of God."* This is NOT an admonition about appropriate behavior in religious buildings. Rather, it is about the behavior of believers in their lives.

How are we as believers to behave? Paul teaches us to behave as who we are! We are in the Body of Christ, God's *living* church. We are to behave accordingly!

Christ Manifest!

This way, the God Who lives within us can be manifested out through our flesh (*i.e.,* His temple).

But we have this treasure in earthen vessels, that the excellency of the power may be of God, and not of us … Always bearing about in the body the dying of the Lord Jesus, that the life

also of Jesus might be manifest in our body. … that the life also of Jesus might be made manifest in our mortal flesh (II Corinthians 4:7, 10-11).

Christ Magnified!

Paul did not stop there – with Christ being *manifest*. His desire was for something even greater: that Christ would be *magnified*.

> *According to my earnest expectation and my hope, that in nothing I shall be ashamed, but that with all boldness, as always, so now also Christ shall be magnified in my body, whether it be by life, or by death* (Philippians 1:20).

We behave ourselves as members of Christ's Body when *He* is manifested and magnified in God's holy temple, *"which temple you are."*

What does the behavior of the believer look like? What does the manifestation and magnification of God's life through Christ look like?

> *But the fruit of the Spirit is love, joy, peace, longsuffering, gentleness, goodness, faith, meekness, temperance* (Galatians 5:22-23).

> *The servant of the Lord must not strive; but be gentle unto all men* (II Timothy 2:24).

> *To speak evil of no man, to be no brawlers, but gentle, showing all meekness unto all men* (Titus 3:2).

> *Walk worthy of the vocation wherewith you are called, with all lowliness and meekness, with longsuffering, forbearing one another in love; endeavoring to keep the unity of the Spirit in the bond of peace* (Ephesians 4:1-3).

> *Put on therefore, as the elect of God, holy and beloved, bowels of mercies, kindness, humbleness of mind, meekness,*

longsuffering; forbearing one another, and forgiving one another, if any man has a quarrel against any: even as Christ forgave you, so also do you. And above all these things put on charity, which is the bond of perfectness (Colossians 3:12-14).

Be kindly affectioned one to another with brotherly love; in honor preferring one another (Romans 12:10).

As we have therefore opportunity, let us do good unto all men, especially unto them who are of the household of faith (Galatians 6:10).

Be not overcome of evil, but overcome evil with good (Romans 12:21).

God lives in you. You are His temple. You are the *"the house of God, which is the church of the living God, the pillar and ground of the truth."*

Behave yourself accordingly!

Appendix 2

Those Turning from the Church Should Turn to Jesus Christ

There is in the world today a great multitude of sincere people who, after giving it a fair trial, have come to the conclusion that they want no part of the religious system that calls itself "the church." They have determined to be free from and live apart from all that travels under this name. They have opted for complete freedom from all organized religion. These are God-fearing men and women who fully believe the biblical record God has given of His Son, the Lord Jesus Christ, so their emancipation declaration has not been so that they will be free to live irresponsible and hedonistic lives. Their highest desire is to live lives of godliness and righteousness in harmony with God's present purpose toward mankind. Many of these have turned irrevocably to the Lord Jesus Christ and are now finding complete satisfaction in Him.

So, on every hand we hear of those who are turning away from every form of organized religion that travels under the canopy of "the church." They say that "the church" has nothing to offer them that they really want, that it does not fulfill their needs, especially their need for a deeper and more accurate knowledge of the Word of God. They see the church structure as being nothing more than a business, run by professional clergymen, whose aim is to get more members, get more money, get greater influence and gain more control. As one man sees it: "Certainly no exegetical talents are needed to quickly discover that most Christian activities have no biblical base. With great sacredness we carry out the ritual of Sunday school, Sunday morning worship, and choir singing accompanied by an instrument better suited for Friday night roller skating. We talk of membership, pledges, reverends, missionaries and Wednesday night prayer meetings as though God had sent some extra-biblical agenda to instruct us how to behave."

As a minister (dispenser) of the Word of God who has no connection with organized religion, I have had much correspondence from priests, pastors and church members (some young, others middle-aged, and many elderly) who state their present disenchantment with the churches with which they have long been associated. They say their denominations are trying to lead them down certain political and social-action paths on which they do not wish to travel, and into certain activities with which they do not wish to be involved. They find many of the "program" and "make-work" activities to be puerile and repugnant, saying that these use up valuable time which could be better spent in other ways.

A church member says, "I went to this church because I was told that the minister was a Bible expositor. This was true, and I enjoyed his messages; but before I knew what was happening or had a chance to refuse, I was made president of the men's bowling league, and this was solely because someone had seen me bowling with my grandson at one of the local alleys. They said it was their way of bringing me into the work. I resigned at once, but since then I have been treated with a coldness which I will no longer endure. So I will soon be on the outside."

"To stir up emotions and create great excitement two or three times a week is the supreme purpose for which my church now exists," a black brother declares. "The minister is expected to serve as a cheerleader to whip up the people, and if enough of them get an emotional high it is declared to have been a wonderful meeting, one on which God has poured out His Spirit. My family and friends love it, and they try to drag me into it, but I think it is bad, very bad, and I am going to protest against it with my feet. ... I'm getting out! Now what do I do? Where do I turn? I'm not an agnostic; I am a Christian, a lover of the Lord Jesus."

My answer to these questions is that it may be for him a very rough road and could even be a lonely road, but all he can do is turn to the Lord Jesus Christ. It is in Him that he will find the true meeting place between God and *man*. It is a difficult position in which he now finds himself, but He will surely find that it is God Who works in him *"both to will and to do of His good pleasure"* (Philippians 2:12-13).

Ever since the days of the so-called "Church fathers" there has been a multitude of Churchmen who have sought to establish, by the process of constant repetition, the idea that Jesus Christ and "the church" are a single package and that you cannot have Christ without taking "the church." They would have us believe that "the churches" are the sole dispensers of Christ and that none can receive Him without coming to them. These errors are constantly repeated every year from many pulpits in thousands of messages under the title of "I Believe in the Church."

In these messages they set forth their accolades concerning "the church," pronouncing their encomiums as to what they believe "the church" to be, then calling upon all hearers to think or believe the same as they do about organizations that call themselves "churches." They take everything praiseworthy that the Spirit of God has said about the *ekklesia* and apply it to *their* "churches."

The many reasons that are being given as causes for turning away from "the churches" are too numerous to be examined in detail. It may be that to take any one of them and segregate it from the rest would make that reason to seem petty and insignificant; but when these are considered in their totality they make up a force that is sweeping many true Christians out of and away from "the churches." The tragedy is that some of these now feel that there is nothing in the future for them but despair and unbelief.

God will never allow anyone to feel satisfied until they find satisfaction in the Lord Jesus Christ. In all my ministry I have never told anyone to leave his "church." However, I will always tell those who are turning away from "the church" that they should turn to the Lord Jesus Christ.

Otis Q. Sellers (edited and abridged)
Seed & Bread (Brief Biblical Messages)
#158 – December 10, 1982

Appendix 3

Christian Individualism:
Life for the Believer in Jesus Christ

declaration of Paul the apostle tells us that all
live godly in Christ Jesus shall suffer persecution
n most lands today, this persecution will usually
dis-fellowshipping, ostracism, separation, and
and misunderstanding of one's high and holy
se same lines, I would add that if anyone does
odly in Christ Jesus, he will have to do it as an
who gives his time searching for some group or
ing godly in Christ Jesus, and to which he may
omed in advance to failure and disappointment.

out Jesus Christ,
ty Save the Written Word of God

ct of living godly in Christ Jesus is that the one
ed has *"chosen the way of truth"* (Psalm 119:30).
sus in saying, *"Thy Word is Truth"* (John 17:17).
been made, the only question that can ever be
teaching or practice is, "Is it the truth?" If it is,
and declared; if not, it must be repudiated.

od in advance that the determination to live
and the choice of "the truth way" rather than
not an easy road to travel. It could be a very
one cannot decide in advance that, through the
e can accept the isolation, the ostracism and
that may come from following such a course,
upon it. He would probably be happier if he
some like-minded group of "food, fun and

fellowship" seekers. If one is going to be miserable living the
a Christian individualist, he had better find some other way of

If, among those who read these lines, there are those who hav
a true encounter with the Lord Jesus Christ; if they have j
themselves as sinners and received Him as their Savior; i
have come face-to-face with the fact of God's Truth versus
error; if they have chosen the way of Truth, and it has becom
determination to grow in grace and in the knowledge of Jesus
– they will find it necessary to find a way of life in Christ Jes
will allow them to live out to the limit the relationship whicl
now bear to God through Him. If Jesus Christ, rather than son
or denomination, is to be the molder of their lives, I recomm
them Christian individualism as being the true and best way
for the active believer in Christ Jesus.

The believer whose knowledge of the Bible is ever increasing,
appreciation of the person and work of Jesus Christ is ever g
with this resulting in a determination to give Him the preen
in all things, will find that he quickly becomes *persona non g*
unacceptable person) in any "church" today. His unwillingne
along with the popular schemes and make-work activities of
religions will cause him to be branded as a divisive factor, a
protests he makes will bring the charge that he is a troublem

The "churches" want bodies to help swell the attendance; th
come purses that will help with the finances, but they insist
erything that means so much to the active believer in Christ
forgotten and left at home. He can play and he can pay, but is
nothing to say. And if he insists in raising his voice in protest
expect a visit from the board of deacons who will insist that
quiet and conform or else face a more drastic action. This can
a frightening prospect to many that they will seek to avoid
cost. So, they become amenable and complacent, usually g
an excuse that they are doing it for the sake of their families.

However, for many others, such compromises are impossi
truth as it is in Christ Jesus means more to them than any orga

and they cannot remain silent when grievous errors and practices are promulgated. Thus, the only course open to them is one of Christian individualism. This means a commitment to Christ and to His Word while standing apart from any commitment to any religious body.

"Without the Church There Is No Christianity"

These are the bold words posted on a "church" sign, a challenge to all who passed by. The one who was responsible for them being there probably believed what they said, and I suppose that many who read them nodded in assent, there being many who would never dare challenge anything written on a "church" sign; but I repudiate and reject them with all the strength of my being.

I am personally acquainted with hundreds who are Christians in every biblical sense that can be given to this exalted word, yet they are Christians wholly apart from all institutions and organizations that are called "churches." In fact, they actually reject "the Christ of the 'churches'" in order that they may fully exalt and give the preeminence to the Christ of the Scriptures.

I claim to be one of these; therefore, I reject the intolerant and dogmatic declaration proclaimed by this "church" sign to all who passed by that without "the church" there is no Christianity.

If this were true it would make the institution called "the church" to be the mediator between man and Christ. It would mean that the life that He would have us live cannot be lived apart from a "church," that he who receives and becomes a part of one must also receive and become a part of the other, and that only those who are identified with some "church" are identified with Christ. All this I repudiate as being contrary to the Word of God.

It has been my joy to recommend Christian individualism as a way of life to many believers in Christ. It is my belief and my experience that it is the privilege of any individual to establish relationship with Jesus Christ in which all that He can ever be to any man in this dispensation, His rich blessings, and fellowship can be enjoyed wholly apart from any institution called a "church." Such things as nearness to God, likeness to Christ, devotedness to His Word, and separation from the world can all be attained and maintained by the individual believer in Jesus Christ without his being any part of an organized company. The believer can be attached to Christ, to His Name, to His Word, yes, even to His people, without being any part of any "church." I offer my own life as proof of this.

These words may come as a shock to many who hold the popular concept that the chief expression of a man's relationship to Christ is to attend a "church" on Sunday morning. Today as a rule men are classified under "those who go to church" and "those who do not go to church." All who go to "church" are considered to be good, honest, moral Christians, and even though this may not be true, men persist in believing this lie. On the other hand, all who do not go to "church" are considered to be heathen unbelievers whose morals are open to question. This is a greater falsehood than a fact.

While it is true that many sincere and true believers in Jesus Christ are found in the "churches," there is no need for me to follow them there in order to have their friendship and enjoy their fellowship. To submit or defer to an organization where, as a rule, matters of great spiritual importance are settled by a majority vote is too high a price for me to pay for the friendship and fellowship of any man. The true believer in Jesus Christ should never deny friendship and fellowship to another believer just because he does not cast his lot with a "church" organization. The sectarian minded will do this, but the fellowship of such is hardly worth having if some surrender of principle must be made to gain it.

Most of my readers, I am sure, are quite familiar with the pressure that in this day is brought upon people to join a "church." It is much easier to yield to this pressure and join up than it is to withstand it and stay out. Vigorous programs of visitation evangelism are carried on in order that membership roles may show a gain, the Sunday services may be better attended, and the budget may be balanced. Men are pressured into putting on "the form of godliness" and becoming members of a "church."

Christian individualism is not for those business and professional men who know the value of the contacts they can make in a "church" organization, nor is it for those who are seeking for community or neighborhood acceptance and approval by belonging to the right organizations, one of which must be the right "church." This is not for the status seekers, nor is it for those who value so highly the "country-club religion" provided by so many "churches" today.

Christian individualism is for the active believer in Jesus Christ who has discovered that his interest in God's truth, and his growth in the knowledge of Jesus Christ has brought him into conflict with the status quo that is so fervently maintained by the organizations that call themselves "churches."

By the term "active believer" I do not necessarily mean a believer who is an active worker. In fact the active believer may find it very difficult to do much work. One of the most difficult things he will face, and must accept as part of his lot in Christ, is the limitation which "living for Christ" is going to force upon him in regard to those activities which so many engage in under the guise of Christian service.

Since faith in Jesus Christ is belief in the record God has given of His Son, the active believer is one who is never satisfied with his knowledge and understanding of God's record. Credal statements concerning Christ may satisfy many, but they do not satisfy the active believer. "That I may know Him" is the motive behind his perpetual and progressive studies in the Word of God.

The words "individualism" and "individualist" have no fixed meaning until they are given a context. If any should turn these words against me and make them to mean egoism and egotist, they will have to ignore the prefix Christian which I always place before these words.

There are many egotists today who are motivated by an excessive love and thought for themselves with a complete disregard for the feelings and wishes of others. My individualism is something that is reserved almost entirely for the Lord Jesus Christ. It is for His glory, not mine.

The primary value of Christian individualism is that it permits a faithful presentation of Jesus Christ to others. It permits one's eye to be single when he seeks to win men to Christ. There is no demand upon him to bring men to Christ and also into some "church." He is able to plead God's cause and feels no need of pleading the cause of any "church" or denomination.

Christian individualism lifts a man to a position of sublime independence of all the religions of this world. The Christian individualist knows that a man can be joined to God through Jesus Christ, and that he does not need to face or become involved in all the divergent issues created by religious organizations. He knows the satisfying value of having gone directly to God, knowing no intermediary but Jesus Christ, His Son, and no other authority save the written Word of God. He smilingly refuses the officious cries of churchmen who declare that he cannot have Christ as his Savior until he has first acknowledged and received them.

The Christian faith was from the very first the personal faith of individuals. This is clearly seen in the declaration of Paul who tells us that after God's dealings with him on the Damascus road, he did not confer with any human being. Neither did he go up to Jerusalem to them who were apostles before him; but he went into Arabia, then later came back to Damascus (see Galatians 1:15-19).

The believers of the Acts period were not always scattered and, wherever possible, they moved and acted as a fellowship of individuals. When one of them found himself cut off from all others, he stood alone, finding his all in Christ.

Before determining to live godly in Christ Jesus, before choosing the way of truth, before starting out on the path of Christian individualism, the believer had better make sure that he can "go it alone" spiritually. It may be necessary for him to do this. Let him be determined in advance that he is able to say with godly Asaph of old: *"Whom have I in heaven but Thee? and there is none upon earth that I desire beside Thee"* (Psalm 73:25).

Christian individualism is a way of life, not a way of escape. It consists of that which an active believer in Christ does, not what he does not do. Let no one take this high and holy position unless his life is to be lived for the glory of Jesus Christ.

Christian individualism does not mean that the believer stands alone; but it does mean that he knows how to stand alone, and that he will without complaint stand happily alone if he deems it to be a part of the worthy walk of his calling. He does not need to look to the right or to the left to see what someone else is going to do. He has a profound sense of his personal responsibility to God, therefore, he will put Him first and every other consideration must be subservient.

While he earnestly desires fellowship and community with others, he refuses to allow this desire to be the reigning influence of his life. He dislikes isolation and aloneness as much as anyone, yet he will not compromise in order to belong. He cannot yield allegiance to any organization, since all organizations are composed of human beings who err and whose judgments are always less than divine truth. …

There are active believers in Jesus Christ who are members of "churches" and who have found a place of service within its membership. Some of these feel that they have solved the great problem of how an individual can also be a member of a group and secure all the benefits of both ways of life. This is their right as an individual. I neither commend this nor condemn it. A believer's right to freedom certainly gives him the right to unite with a group. However, a difficulty arises when he begins to think that it is the duty of others to do the same, and it needs to be recognized that individualism has ceased when a man's acceptance by a group is based upon his silence.

"How Can Anyone Worship if He Does Not Go to Church?"

This is the question often asked. This query does nothing more than reveal the ignorance of the one who asks it concerning the meaning and character of true worship. Here is another *quid pro quo* which would make worship to be that which men do in "church" on Sunday, therefore, he who does not attend church does not worship. This is denied.

True worship is always a personal and individual matter which, while it may be done with a company, it will not be done at all unless it is done by an individual. True worship is heartfelt adoration of God because of who He is, what He is and what He does. It is not dependent upon place or ritual. It needs no established forms or ceremonies. Whenever because of revealed truth a heart responds with adoration and gratitude because of what God is or what He has done, that is worship.

Quite a few believers who have considered Christian individualism as a way of life have asked about fellowship with other believers. To this there is only one answer – fellowship with others to the very limit. Christian individualism is not an anti-social way of life.

So, after all has been said, and all arguments pro and con have been exhausted, there is only one method of dealing with God in this dispensation; that method is personally and individually. This is the way we must start, this is the way we should continue. In this way of life, we can best fulfill our position as believers in an unbelieving world as students of God's Word in a world that is biblically illiterate.

Otis Q. Sellers
(*Edited and Abridged*)

Appendix 4

Not Forsaking the Assembling of Ourselves Together

Not forsaking the assembling of ourselves together, as the manner of some is; but exhorting one another: and so much the more, as ye see the day approaching (Hebrews 10:25).

The usual interpretation of this passage associates it with attendance at a Christian place of worship.

The word *"assembling"* (*episunagoge*), and its cognate (*episunago*), are never used of an *"assembling"* in the sense of attending service at church … The only other place where *episunagoge* occurs is II Thessalonians 2:1.

> *The coming of our Lord Jesus Christ, and our **gathering together** unto Him.*

The apostle, by the use of the word *"forsaking"* evidently glances back to such passages as II Chronicles 24:18, where the *"forsaking"* of the house of the Lord meant *apostasy,* and was visited with wrath, and also to Nehemiah 10:39 and 13:11, where adherence to the house of God indicated loyalty. The *"gathering together of ourselves"* has value only as it foreshadows the hope of *"our gathering together unto Him."* At the present time faithfulness to truth and to the blessed hope sometimes cuts us off from Christian assemblies, and this passage must never be used to justify compromise. The present Dispensation knows no "place of worship" except where *"Christ sitteth at the right hand of God,"* for God *"dwelleth not in temples made with hands"* …

The added words, *"so much the more, as ye see the day approaching,"* confirms the thought that the hope and its gathering together is all the while in view.

A further confirmation of this higher and fuller meaning is found in the argument that immediately follows. The forsaking of the assembly is called a *"willful sin after the reception of the truth,"* and for such *"there remaineth no more sacrifice for sins."*

Under the law sins were placed under two heads:

(1) Sins of omission, ignorance and inadvertence (Levticus 4:2, etc.).

(2) Sins of presumption, high hand, malice aforethought (Numbers 15:30-31).

Apostasy from the profession of the hope had the character of presumptuous sin, for which the law made no provision. That David (as in Psalm 51), for example, could be forgiven, shows that a fuller Sacrifice is found under the gospel than under the law, but the apostle does not bring this forward, neither does he mitigate the severity of the judgment that is pronounced against such.

"Fiery indignation, which shall devour the adversaries," "died without mercy," "of how much sorer punishment," "vengeance is Mine," "it is a fearful thing to fall into the hands of the living God" – all stress the extreme severity of the penalty. *"Trodden under foot the Son of God," "counting the blood of the Covenant unholy," "doing despite to the Spirit of grace"* – these terms reveal the enormity of the sin of turning back to Judaism.

In this light, Hebrews 6:1-8 is to be read, to which the word *"illuminated"* of 10:32 evidently refers. These are the only occurrences of *photizo* in Hebrews.

Charles H. Welch (1888-1967)
Perfection or Perdition: *An Exposition of the Epistle to the Hebrews,* Page 156

Your Part

Now that you have read this book, it's your turn.

If the truths presented here have helped you, don't let these truths die in your hands.

Please write to us and let us know your thoughts concerning its content.

Consider assisting us in getting this book into the hands of those who would be encouraged and strengthened by its message:

- Recommend it to your friends and loved ones.

- Order additional copies to give as gifts.

- Keep extra copies on hand to loan to others.

If you have not read the author's other works, order them today.

We would be honored to have your fellowship in getting this book freely to those who hunger spiritually. We have daily opportunities to send it to pastors, Sunday school teachers, Bible college professors and students, Bible class teachers, and prisoners.

StudyShelf.com™
Powered by Pilkington and Sons

Your source for rare and hard-to-find Bible study materials for the serious minded, hungry-hearted students of Scripture.

Over the years we have been often asked to recommend books. The requests come from believers who longed for material with substance. Study Shelf™ is a collection of books which are, in our opinion, the very best in print. Many of these books are "unknown" to the members of the Body of Christ at large, and most are not available at your local "Christian" bookstore.

Some of Our Authors	*Some of Our Topics*
Sir Robert Anderson	Alcohol
T. Austin-Sparks	Baptism
Charles F. Baker	Church History
E.W. Bullinger	Commentaries
H.A. Ironside	Dispensational
A.E. Knoch	Exchanged Life
Clarence Larkin	Gap Theory
C.H. Mackintosh	Government
William R. Newell	Home
J.C. O'Hair	Racism
C.R. Stam	Reference
Miles Stanford	Spiritual Growth
Charles Welch	Universal Reconciliation
Martin Zender	War

PILKINGTON & SONS
PO Box 265 Windber, PA 15963
www.studyshelf.com
1-800-784-6010

Do You Subscribe to the Bible Student's Notebook™?

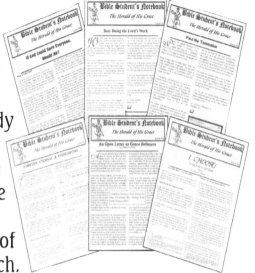

This is a periodical that ...

- Promotes the study of the Bible.
- Encourages the growth of the believer in grace.
- Supports the role of the family patriarch.
- Is dedicated to the recovery of truth that has too long been hidden under the veils of traditionalism, prejudice, misunderstanding and fear.
- Is not connected with any "Movement," "Organization," "Mission," or separate body of believers, but is sent forth to and for all saints.

The *Bible Student's Notebook™* is published weekly.

DAILY EMAIL GOODIES™

Do you receive our
Daily Email Goodies™?

These are free daily emails that contain short quotes, articles, and studies on Biblical themes.

These are the original writings of Clyde L. Pilkington, Jr, as well as gleanings from other authors.

<u>Here is what our readers are saying</u>:

"Profound! Comforting! Calming! Wonderful!" – NC

"The Daily Email Goodies continue to bless my heart! ... They provide plenty of food for thought." – IL

"I really appreciate the Goodies!" – VA

"Your Daily Email Goodies are making me aware of authors whose names I don't even know." – GA

"I am glad to be getting the Daily Email Goodies – keep 'em coming." – IN

Request to be added to our free
Daily Email Goodies™

If you would like to be added to the mailing list, email us at:
Goodies@StudyShelf.com

www.URQA.com

Universal Reconciliation

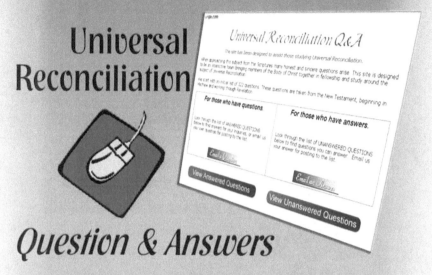

Question & Answers

A website designed to assist those studying Universal Reconciliation.

When approaching this subject from the Scriptures many honest and sincere questions arise. This site is designed to be an interactive forum bringing members of the Body of Christ together in fellowship and study around the subject of Universal Reconciliation.

We start with an initial list of 322 questions. These questions are taken from the New Testament, beginning in Matthew and working through Revelation.

For those who have questions:

Look through a list of ANSWERED QUESTIONS to find answers for your inquiries, or email us your own question for posting to the list.

For those who have answers:

Look through a list of UNANSWERED QUESTIONS to find questions you can answer. Email us your answers for posting to the list.

Stop by www.urqa.com
Today!

The Salvation of ALL – Creation's Final Destination

(A Biblical Look at Universal Reconciliation)

The Gospel of our Lord and Savior, Jesus Christ is truly better "Good News" than we could ever have imagined. It is far more glorious than religion would ever have us believe. The Salvation of All is a book about a "Good News" that will reach its final goal in the salvation of all mankind.

(#7001) 262 pages, PB.

Study Shelf
PO Box 265, Windber, PA 15963
www.StudyShelf.com
1-800-784-6010

I Choose! *Living Life to Its Fullest*

Forty-Eight Daily Thoughts on Divine Life

You are alive! Yet not just alive, but alive with the very life of God! Don't allow your "What if …" imaginations of the past or the future to lay claim to the present that God has given you. Allow the objective, unchanging truth of who God has made you in the Lord Jesus Christ to transform your mind and life as you take this spiritual journey of **"I Choose."**

(#4120) 192 pages, PB.

Study Shelf
PO Box 265, Windber, PA 15963
www.StudyShelf.com
1-800-784-6010

Except the Lord build the house, they labor in vain that build it (Psalms 127:1).

This book represents many years of work. The author believes that it is one of the most important books that he will ever be privileged to write, simply because it is about one of the most vital scriptural subjects that could ever be addressed.

The home is central to all of God's dealings with man throughout the course of time. It is His Divine "institution" and "organization" upon the earth; and for the believer, it is the *Embassy of Heaven*. An embassy is **"the residence or office of an ambassador."** Since the believer is an ambassador of the Lord Jesus Christ (II Corinthians 5:14-21), his home is thus the *Divine Embassy* of heavenly ministry.

Pauline ministry is centered in the homes of believers. This is even the true sphere of the Body of Christ; for this reason our apostle speaks of *"church in thy house."* This book doesn't focus upon the *external* specifics of the ministry of *Heaven's Embassy* (such as *hospitality*); that will be saved for another volume. Instead, it looks at the inner-workings of the *Embassy* itself, focusing upon its very nature and *internal* purpose and function.

Heaven's Embassy
The Divine Plan and Purpose of the Home

(#5675) 250 pages, PB.

Study Shelf
PO Box 265, Windber, PA 15963
www.StudyShelf.com
1-800-784-6010

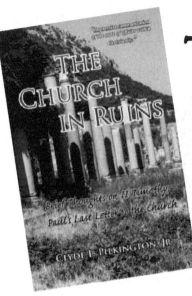

THE CHURCH IN RUINS

Brief Thoughts on II Timothy, Paul's Last Letter to the Church

This brief survey of Paul's last epistle will reveal that while almost 2000 years have transpired, the condition of the church has remained the same, and indeed has worsened in accordance with Paul's warning to Timothy.

This book is not a call for a re-awakening of "the church," because it is apparent that this is not Father's plan. Rather, it is a call to individual men – men whose place in the Christian religious system has left them empty, stagnant, and restless – to awaken to Father's call to be His faithful servant and stand outside of that system to look for other faithful men as well.

Appendix 3

Christian Individualism:
A Way of Life for the Believer in Jesus Christ

The God-inspired declaration of Paul the apostle tells us that all who determine to live godly in Christ Jesus shall suffer persecution (II Timothy 3:12). In most lands today, this persecution will usually take the form of dis-fellowshipping, ostracism, separation, and misrepresentation and misunderstanding of one's high and holy purpose. Along these same lines, I would add that if anyone does determine to live godly in Christ Jesus, he will have to do it as an individual. The one who gives his time searching for some group or company that is living godly in Christ Jesus, and to which he may attach himself, is doomed in advance to failure and disappointment.

No Intermediary but Jesus Christ,
No Other Authority Save the Written Word of God

A most positive aspect of living godly in Christ Jesus is that the one who has so determined has *"chosen the way of truth"* (Psalm 119:30). He joins the Lord Jesus in saying, *"Thy Word is Truth"* (John 17:17). Once this choice has been made, the only question that can ever be asked concerning any teaching or practice is, "Is it the truth?" If it is, it must be embraced and declared; if not, it must be repudiated.

It should be understood in advance that the determination to live godly in Christ Jesus, and the choice of "the truth way" rather than "the church way" is not an easy road to travel. It could be a very lonesome road. So, if one cannot decide in advance that, through the help of Jesus Christ, he can accept the isolation, the ostracism and the misunderstanding that may come from following such a course, he had better not start upon it. He would probably be happier if he simply cast his lot with some like-minded group of "food, fun and fellowship" seekers. If one is going to be miserable living the life of a Christian individualist, he had better find some other way of life.

If, among those who read these lines, there are those who have had a true encounter with the Lord Jesus Christ; if they have judged themselves as sinners and received Him as their Savior; if they have come face-to-face with the fact of God's Truth versus man's error; if they have chosen the way of Truth, and it has become their determination to grow in grace and in the knowledge of Jesus Christ – they will find it necessary to find a way of life in Christ Jesus that will allow them to live out to the limit the relationship which they now bear to God through Him. If Jesus Christ, rather than some sect or denomination, is to be the molder of their lives, I recommend to them Christian individualism as being the true and best way of life for the active believer in Christ Jesus.

The believer whose knowledge of the Bible is ever increasing, whose appreciation of the person and work of Jesus Christ is ever growing, with this resulting in a determination to give Him the preeminence in all things, will find that he quickly becomes *persona non grata* (an unacceptable person) in any "church" today. His unwillingness to go along with the popular schemes and make-work activities of today's religions will cause him to be branded as a divisive factor, and any protests he makes will bring the charge that he is a troublemaker.

The "churches" want bodies to help swell the attendance; they welcome purses that will help with the finances, but they insist that everything that means so much to the active believer in Christ must be forgotten and left at home. He can play and he can pay, but is allowed nothing to say. And if he insists in raising his voice in protest, he can expect a visit from the board of deacons who will insist that he keep quiet and conform or else face a more drastic action. This can be such a frightening prospect to many that they will seek to avoid it at any cost. So, they become amenable and complacent, usually giving as an excuse that they are doing it for the sake of their families.

However, for many others, such compromises are impossible. The truth as it is in Christ Jesus means more to them than any organization,